Modern Traditions

Klaus-Peter Gast

Modern Traditions
Contemporary Architecture in India

Birkhäuser
Basel · Boston · Berlin

―**Graphic Design**
Miriam Bussmann, Berlin

―**Lithography**
Licht+Tiefe, Berlin

―**CAD assistance**
Raphel Kalapurakkal, Cochin

―**Printing**
Freiburger Graphische Betriebe, Freiburg i. Br.

This book is also available in a German language edition:
ISBN 978-3-7643-7753-3

Bibliographic information published by the Deutsche Nationalbibliothek
The Deutsche Nationalbibliothek lists this publication in the Deutsche
Nationalbibliografie; detailed bibliographic data are available in the
Internet at <http://dnb.ddb.de>.

Library of Congress Control Number: 2007922517

This work is subject to copyright. All rights are reserved, whether
the whole or part of the material is concerned, specifically the
rights of translation, reprinting, re-use of illustrations, recitation,
broadcasting, reproduction on microfilms or in other ways, and
storage in data banks. For any kind of use, permission of the
copyright owner must be obtained.

© 2007 Birkhäuser Verlag AG
Basel · Boston · Berlin
P.O.Box 133, CH-4010 Basel, Switzerland
Part of Springer Science+Business Media
Printed on acid-free paper produced from chlorine-free pulp. TCF ∞

Printed in Germany

ISBN 978-3-7643-7754-0

9 8 7 6 5 4 3 2 1

www.birkhauser.ch

Table of Contents

7	**Foreword** Raj Jadhav	15	**The Waking Giant**

— MODERN INDIAN

26   Charles Correa and Associates
Vidhan Bhavan Government Building
Bhopal, 1997

34   Rahul Mehrotra and Associates
House in a Plantation
Ahmedabad, 2004

42   Raj Rewal and Associates
Indian Parliament Library
New Delhi, 2003

— REGIONALISTIC-MODERN

50   Shimul Javeri Kadri Architects
Production Building for Synergy Lifestyles
Karur, 2004

— LATE MODERN

60   HCP Design and Project Management Pvt. Ltd.
**Indian Institute of Management
New Campus (IIM)**
Ahmedabad, 2006

68   Charles Correa and Associates
Town Planning
Mumbai and Bagalkot, under construction

— MINIMAL-ECONOMICAL

74   Raj Rewal and Associates
CIDCO Lowcost Housing
New Mumbai, 1993

— CLASSICAL-MODERN

82   Khareghat and Associates
Belvedere and Tytan Apartment Blocks
Mumbai, under construction

88   Klaus-Peter Gast
House Leslie Pallath
Cochin, 2005

— MATERIAL-TEXTURAL

96   Rahul Mehrotra and Associates
Accommodation for the Tata Institute of Social Sciences
Tuljapur, 2000

— TRADITIONAL

104   Shimul Javeri Kadri Architects
Ayushakti – Ayurvedic Treatment Clinic
Mumbai, 1999

110   Karl Damschen
Brunton Boatyard Hotel
Cochin, 1999

— ECOLOGICAL-SUSTAINABLE

118   Karan Grover and Associates
Sohrabji Godrej Green Business Center
Hyderabad, 2003

128   Selected Bibliography   128   Illustrations Credits

Much of contemporary Indian architecture, though modern in expression, is rooted in its millennia-old past. Unlike modern architecture of the West, which started in a "clean slate" environment after the widespread destruction of the world wars, the architecture of India, over the thousands of years of its existence, is a temporal progression with many interventions that served as modifiers. The process of inquiry has been long and tedious with deep self-examination of established conventions in an attempt to accommodate the interventions. Hence, architecture of every era in the history of Indian architecture is an expression of its time, and yet, is rooted in its past. To understand contemporary Indian architecture, therefore, it is necessary to understand the determinants and causes of architectural methods and expression in India today.

In the West today, technology is an integral part of its worldview. In fact, technology determines process and production, and process and production determine technology. The "clean slate" environment and its causes enabled the West to look to the future with vigour. Technology enabled the West to go into the unknown, creating a new form of architecture. Today, technology determines much of architectural production and explorations. Romi Khosla calls these explorations "abstract futures[1]" where "dynamism and movement" are the primary impulses of the Western world. The pre-modern past plays a lesser role, if any.

The East, on the other hand, is characterised by its connections with the past and its imperatives of appropriating the dynamic of modernism into its temporal progression. Modernism cannot be ignored in the East and is implicitly accepted as the inevitable future direction, primarily because of its colonial history, and also because of the inter-dependency and emerging homogenising tendencies of the world. The countries of the East are now inextricably part of the modern world. The challenge, therefore, is to reconcile their ancient past with the spirit, systems, methods and products of the modern world. It is from this viewpoint that we need to read the contents of this book.

Plurality in the Indian context The core of Indianness lies in spirituality and related ancient myths. It is widely acknowledged that the spirit of tolerance is rooted in the origins of Indian civilisation, particularly in its spiritual discourse. Hence, it was possible for numerous schools of thought to originate and co-exist simultaneously. Hinduism as a worldview[2] co-existed with Buddhism, Jainism and other spiritual systems that emerged as alternatives to Hindu thought. The architecture of each of these schools of thought was expressive of their views and determined by cosmological connotations, myth and discourse depicted as narratives in sculptural form, and a general allusion to the holistic and integrative worldview of their time. Complex ancient Indian art

—**Foreword**
Raj Jadhav

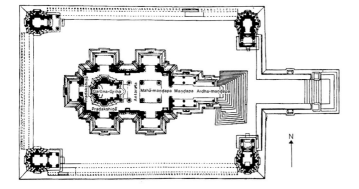

Plan of a northern Indian temple

Northern Indian temple ⎯ Fatehpur Sikri ⎯ Administration building, Mumbai ⎯ Art Deco cinema, Mumbai

theories formed the foundation of much of the production of architecture.

When Persian invaders arrived from the 7th century AD onward, their worldview was significantly different from the existing worldviews. Opulence, narratives in the form of Quranic verses inscribed on edifices, ostentation, Persian form and aesthetics marked this new intervention. Depiction of humans and animals was forbidden – an axiom exactly opposite to the sculptural narratives of the pre-Islamic cultures. A number of other differences emerged. For almost a thousand years up to the 18th century, the Islamic and pre-Islamic architectures co-existed. The people learned to live with their differences or tried to harmonise them. Despite these differences, there were attempts at reconciliation between the Islamic and the pre-Islamic expressions. Moghul emperor Akbar's city of Fatehpur Sikri, built in the 16th century, is a representative example of such an attempted reconciliation.

European colonialists arrived gradually from around the 17th century bringing with them a third disparate worldview of Cartesian rationality, the Christian religion and European Classicism with its descendent styles. Architecture became a statement of imperial power with its grandeur and stylistic elements. Local craftsmen skilled in millennia-old traditions of craft were re-trained in the European arts. Colonial architecture became another addition to the plurality of architecture in India. The Modern thought was brought to India by the British Raj, bringing with it new materials, technology, methods and processes. The demise of the millennia-old traditions of craft became inevitable. Architecture was no longer produced by srenis (guilds) of mistris (craftsmen), but by architects and engineers who designed on drawing boards and never handled the material used for construction.

The Art Deco style is an important expression of modern architecture of the early to mid-20th century. A large number of buildings were built in this style well into the 1960s. After 1947 in independent India, Jawarharlal Nehru, educated in England, turned to Le Corbusier to initiate an architectural model that was reflective of Nehru's vision of an industrialised India. Le Corbusier's design for the city of Chandigarh became the symbol of modern Indian architecture. At the time, India followed the socialist model of governance and embarked upon huge infrastructure projects, which included the construction of government office buildings and residential schemes. Corbusian modernism was unquestioningly adopt-ed for more than two decades.

It was only in the 1980s that modernism in its Corbusian avatar was recognised as being inadequate to address the realities of Indian society. The ancient Indian past could not be ignored in architecture because the ancient past is also its living present. Modernism needed to be appropriated to the temporal progression of the ancient past. Hence, architects like Raj Rewal, Charles Correa, Balkrishna Doshi and others attempted to reconcile modern architecture with prevailing identifications of Indianness bringing about a "modern Indian" architecture – another idea in the field of architectural expressions over the millennia of Indian civilisation.

Meanwhile, architectural exploration within the modernist realm continued in different parts of the country. The Matrimandir in Auroville designed by Roger Anger displayed a spiritual ideology, as do a number of other buildings there. Laurie Baker's work in Kerala is low cost, self-help, culturally and climatically responsive as can be seen in his Center for Developmental Studies. Satish Gujral's Belgian embassy building in New Delhi is sculptural with connotations of Hindu myth. These are just a few examples of the diversity of modern architecture in India built in the last couple of decades or so.

A major event in Indian history took place in 1991 when the government abandoned the socialist project in favour of a liberalised economy, integrating the Indian economy with global realities. This "liberalisation" had a huge impact upon urban Indian architecture. Corporate architecture connected with global finance became a significant chunk of architectural activity with its glass and aluminum façades and universalised expressions. Architecture of the retail industry, too, became a significant part of construction activity. Architecture in India was now being governed by economic globalisation. The era of socialism with its state-controlled production

Jawahar Kala Kendra arts center, Jaipur, Charles Correa — Hiranandani Gardens

mechanisms was gone. Demand, supply, and profitability became the determinants of architecture.

Alongside the architecture of corporate and retail buildings there is another huge industry of housing. Migration to urban centres increases the demand for residential accommodation, raising prices of property significantly. Residential property developers are growing in number and packaging their buildings to attract buyers. Ornamentation derived from classical European architecture adorns huge residential buildings. In cities like Mumbai such buildings are fairly commonplace. Hiranandani Gardens by architect Hafeez Contractor is one such project.

Simultaneously, the ideas of modern Indian architecture continue to exist as do traditional architectural expressions (in religious buildings and rural dwellings). A number of other expressions contribute to the creation of a rich plurality in the built environment of India. In my opinion, if not for the spiritual concept of tolerance of ancient India such rich plurality would not exist. This ancient spiritual concept of tolerance will continue to be open to interventions in the future while adapting them to suit the Indian user. Furthermore, with the Indian government's acceptance of World Trade Organisation's General Agreement on Trade in Services (GATS), the country is now open to foreign architects to practice. This will add to the plurality, making Indian architecture more diverse and exciting.

The socio-cultural determinant In his book *House Form and Culture*[3], Amos Rapoport argues that house form is principally determined by socio-cultural factors of the parent society, and then by pragmatic considerations of economics, climate, materials, technology and so on. It appears that a large part of architecture in India follows this theory. The ancient Indian architectural text of Vastu Shastra is widely used in modern Indian architecture for planning houses, residential complexes, office, commercial, industrial and other building types.

The principles of Vastu Shastra regulate planning and design specifics from town planning to the furniture layout of a room. The stipulations are said to be governed by ancient empirical knowledge of the human body and its relation to the earth and the cosmos. Following these stipulations, it is said, ensures overall human well-being. Hence, a client with a belief in Vastu Shastra will choose a plot of land and locate the functions and elements of a building using the guidelines of this text. Architects and clients consult specialists in Vastu Shastra and then agree upon a design. The belief in this ancient body of knowledge is experiencing a rapid revival.

Raj Rewal offers another approach to socio-cultural architectural design in his work. Rewal has identified six elements of traditional architecture that are multi-functional in purpose, i.e. they are social and cultural spaces, climatically responsive and traditionally icons of community identity. The urban fabric, building clusters, courtyards, streets, *darwaza* (the gateway as an element that defines the inside versus the outside) and roof terraces comprise the six elements. For example, Rewal uses the courtyard as a place where social encounters and cultural activities may take place. Additionally, the courtyard is a light well and an effective ventilation strategy for hot and dry climates. In the Central Institute for Educational Technology at New Delhi, Rewal abstracts a traditional *chhatri* (an architectural kiosk on the terrace for panoramic views) into a modern aesthetic exemplifying the traditional icon of local identity.

Rewal alludes to the ancient Indian art theory of rasa – a Sanskrit word that approximates the English word "flavour" but in a more heightened sense. It should not be confused with "character." The idea of rasa in architecture may be interpreted as an insertion of a singular and unique quality in experiential aesthetics, which is in conformity with and adds to the function and purpose of the building. The intention is to make architecture not only functional but also responsive to the visual and tactile senses in a way that conforms to the function of the building. The incorporation of this idea of rasa also makes a connenction to the culture of the past. Other architects, like Charles Correa, prefer to use cultural iconography in their buildings. For the Jawahar Kala Kendra at Jaipur, for example, he used a mandala (a geometrical representation of the world[4]) of nine squares abstracted as a plan, and large imagery of ancient Hindu myth.

Central Institute of Educational Technology (CIET), New Delhi

Sohrabji Godrej Green Business Center, Hyderabad

Socio-cultural design is widely prevalent in the folk architecture[5] of rural India. For example, the role of women in society determines women's areas in a house. The decorative patterns and colours used to adorn a house have deep cultural significance. Some of these adornments are used in urban Indian houses, too. Socio-cultural elements and spaces continue to play an important role in determining architecture in India. This strong Indian identification forms an integral part of traditional and modern architecture in India.

Sustainable architecture – an ancient Indian tradition

Ancient Indian spiritual thought integrates humans with the cosmos presenting an understanding that the processes of the cosmos are directly related to human existence. With this understanding, ancient Indian civilisation has always respected its environment. Typical principles include climate-responsive design, use of local materials, use of sustainable materials, water harvesting and others. Climate-responsive architectural design is especially sophisticated with thousands of years of refinement. Unfortunately, this knowledge seems to have lost its significance in the last 50 years or so.

Today, however, a number of architects are combining traditional methods and principles of sustainable design with modern methods and principles. One example of such a combination is Karan Grover's CII Sohrabji Godrej Green Business Center (CII-Godrej GBC) at Hyderabad. The building combines traditional Indian design principles of sustainable architecture with the United States Green Building Council's (USGBC) Leadership in Energy and Environmental Design (LEED version 2) framework. A number of traditional Indian principles of sustainable design already are included in the LEED framework like the use of local and sustainable materials and water harvesting. Other traditional principles used by Grover include the use of wind towers for catching wind, tunneling it through its shaft, thus cooling and treating it (artificially, in the case of the CII-Godrej GBC) before circulating it in habitable spaces.

The design around a courtyard is another traditional climate-responsive feature. The courtyard helps in reducing the use of artificial lighting, creates shade due to the building mass and facilitates stack ventilation.[6] It is CII-Godrej GBC's objective to collaborate with the USGBC to modify the LEED framework with Indian knowledge input so that it may be applied to Indian conditions. Also, it is CII-Godrej GBC's objective to propagate the revised LEED framework within India and Asia in an effort to make the CII-Godrej GBC's initiative the centre of Asian green building activity[7]. With such intentions, sustainable building design is being institutionalised in modern architecture of India today. Obviously, the future of modern Indian architecture is likely to be green in design.

Conclusion Due to their spiritual and cultural grounding, millennia-old architectural principles continue today and will continue well into the future. I have identified plurality of architectural design, socio-cultural determinants and sustainable design as significant features of the past, the present and the future of Indian architecture. The pluralistic nature of contemporary Indian architecture makes it an exciting field for future explorations and innovations. Socio-cultural determinants are "Indianising" modern and universalised architecture, thus helping a modern Indian architectural identity evolve. India is bound to become the centre of modern sustainable architecture in Asia.

I find all three features very encouraging for the future of Indian architecture. Klaus-Peter Gast's book must be read with this background in mind, as it aims to capture these and other features of contemporary Indian architecture. Gast's collection of projects is representative of today's and tomorrow's Indian architectural directions, which are unique in that India's past is a living reality that, most likely, will also shape the future of India's architecture. Klaus-Peter Gast's book will benefit anybody interested in the contemporary architecture of India.

---

1 Khosla, Romi. *The loneliness of a Long Distant Future: Dilemmas of Contemporary Architecture*. New Delhi: Tulika, 2002.
2 Hinduism came to be identified as a religion only after the faith of Islam came into India in the 8th century AD. See Singh, Jaswant. *A Call to Honour: In Service of Emergent India*. New Delhi: Rupa & Co. 2006, p. 82.
3 Rapoport, Amos. *House Form and Culture*. NJ: Prentice-Hall, Inc., 1969.
4 Lang, Jon, Desai, Madhavi, Desai, Miki. *Architecture and Independence: The Search for Identity – India 1880 to 1980*. Delhi: Oxford University Press, 1997.
5 I use Amos Rapoport's understanding of the term "folk architecture", which alludes to architecture of the common people. See Rapoport, Amos. *House Form and Culture*. NJ: Prentice-Hall, Inc., 1969. p.2.
6 Jadhav, Rajratna. www.architectureweek.com/2004/0922/environment_1-1.html
7 www.greenbusinesscentre.org/grn/events/

At midnight on 14 August 1947, India's first prime minister Jawaharlal Nehru proclaimed "the ending of poverty and ignorance and disease and inequality of opportunity."[1] India had gained her independence after over 200 years of British rule. Mohandas Karamchand (Mahatma) Gandhi's compassionately non-violent struggle against repression and occupation of a once free nation had been a triumphant success. Since the 16th century, at the time of the Muslim conqueror Akbar, the people of the sub-continent had been tolerant and ready to communicate, able to live together, vigorously active and ready to exchange ideas. From time immemorial, pluralism and the acceptance of many different ways of thinking had been part of a country that called itself Bharat and later Hindustan, derived from the river Indus. This part of the world had had to tolerate conquest not just since the time of Akbar, but even since the days of Alexander the Great, but it usually responded with astonishing calm and lack of violence. India always absorbed new things that came upon her unbidden, and used them for her own ends. Things alien became Indian and part of the national heritage. This is where Indian globalisation began, earlier than in any other country, without Indians ever having passed beyond their own borders: India was anti-imperial and never waged expansionist wars. And so it remains to be asked whether these extraordinary qualities have survived over 200 years of occupation and whether Nehru's emphatic proclamation has become reality 60 years later. The "largest democracy in the world" that is now establishing itself adopted a socialist system modelled upon the Soviet Union, an ideal of justice according to Nehru, with a central command economy based on five year plans. As Gandhi had been assassinated just six months after independence, he was no longer able to introduce his idea of an India of villages, largely self-governed and with small industries. Nehru implemented his ideas uncompromisingly, and relations with the Soviet Union reached their high point. His policies were followed in principle by his daughter Indira Gandhi and later by her son Rajiv Gandhi. The Nehru doctrine was not abandoned until 1992, when a new economic policy was introduced by the then prime minister and former finance minister Manmohan Singh, under prime minister Narasimha Rao. The gateway to the world was opened, the end for self-sufficient economic policies in this mysterious land beyond the Himalayas, then still almost unknown to the rest of the world. When India opened herself up to the global market, this was the second crucial turning-point for the country in the 20th century: individuals regained their old freedom in private and commercial life, and a gigantic, hitherto untapped pool of intelligence has since been able to develop freely and use its creative energy. This laid the foundations for an explosive economic miracle in the last 15 years. Ultra-rapid technological progress started in co-operation with international firms, with foreign concerns suddenly setting new standards. But critical voices were raised as well: could and should India, after having been anchored culturally for millennia, expose herself to influences of this kind? Should the materialistically driven Western world of thought and action become the new standard for an India based on spiritual values? Here, too, a

—**The Waking Giant**

Jawaharlal Nehru

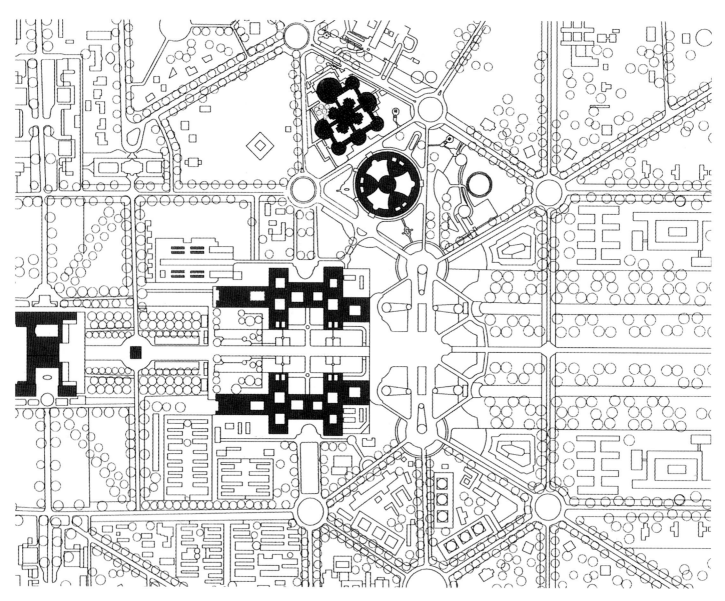

New Delhi, government buildings

degree of calm set in, as each individual's standard of living was and is growing. India will always be in a position in her history to use the new for her own ends, without abandoning her values.

But the desire for global markets led, as in many other countries, to protests against globalisation and the multinationals' expansion of power. This represents an opportunity for a novice to make a very conscious move against this danger of uncontrollable power, offering a personal contribution to a more balanced approach. However, a not inconsiderable social asymmetry has to be set against the large growth rates of 8% at the time of writing and 7% predicted until the year 2025.[2] The caste system, the degenerated hierarchical social structure according to birth, is only one aspect of this, generally there is a lack of willingness to accept anyone in a different social position. A democratic balance operates in politics, but India's social and economic life is rife with imbalance. So a demand must be made for more practical and less theoretical democracy, like for example the realisation of the right to education and employment for all. Women are still the key here: over 60% of them have never attended school. Also, the political response has produced a contrary reaction: the controversial quota regulation for the "scheduled castes", which is intended to help the so-called untouchable caste to a greater legal share of places in education, has led to new social injustices. Rural areas contrast starkly with the big cities in educational matters, and contradict the realities of economic power. Furthermore, the legal system inherited from the British, like the whole bureaucratic system, is an extremely cumbersome piece of machinery, making law and justice unjust and time-consuming: a criminal offence can take about ten years to be dealt with.

The caste system in particular is a spiritual paradox regardless of religion, as everyone is equal before God. This has always been proclaimed in tolerant Hinduism, which is not a religion, but a way of life, as demonstrated for example around 1900 by the monk Swami Vivekananda, who was particularly open to Western countries. About 80% of the Indian population are followers of Hinduism, but they are by no means a homogeneous, strictly disciplined religious community, like for example Islam. In fact it is a multicultural world faith community, of a complexity that is not so easy to grasp, ranging from atheism via the majority of believers to the orthodox-nationalistic Hindutva. While the open-minded, probably the majority of Hindus, are favourably inclined towards the innovation of contemporary Indian society, the orthodox believers, who live according to the strictest rules and traditions, range from sceptical to disapproving. What they all have in common is their reliance on the "primal knowledge" of the Veda, a philosophical moral compendium explaining the cosmos and the world. It has been interpreted in countless ways and was developed many ages ago.

A whole range of religious or even ethnic sub-groups, including Muslims and Christians, live in this land of 250 languages, whose population has just passed the billion mark. With a growth rate of 13 million people per year, it is understandable that diseases which have been eradicated elsewhere like polio, typhoid or malaria are here not so easy to get under control. With a population of this size and so many different groups of people, disintegration could be in the air. But when what was officially the first Indian atomic bomb exploded in the north-western desert area in 1998, this had to be interpreted as part of a national, all-unifying self-confidence. One of the men involved in developing the bomb, the high-ranking scientist Dr. Abdul Kalam, was then elected president of the country. National awareness unites the many different Indians, so the disintegration that was widely predicted after independence, the "balkanisation" of India, never started to come about. The nation stands together today, and Nehru would certainly have acknowledged this with particular pride.

The following part is devoted to the achievements of Modernist architecture in India, as part of the country's great service to culture, performed especially by the philosopher Vivekananda (d. 1902), the poet and Nobel laureate Rabindranath Tagore (d. 1941) and the director Satyajit Ray (d. 1992), among others, with all the impact they made on the 20th century. Then selected examples will introduce the most

New Delhi, view of the government buildings

Calcutta, Victoria Memorial — Mumbai, Victoria Station

recent trends in contemporary architecture as part of the cultural progress that is also feature of India.

The development of Modernist architecture in India The concept of "Modernism" in 20th century Indian architectural development remains difficult to grasp, as it was used within numerous stylistic developments, following the spirit of the day. Starting with the efforts made by Europeans in the 1920s, the idea of "modern architecture" as a revolutionary and innovative force started to make cautious headway in India in the early 1930s. But at that time any Western thought and practice introduced as a British import was seen as "modern", as India had no uniform independent architectural movement in the early 20th century. Ideas influenced by the Bauhaus and Le Corbusier and then brought to India were modern, and the subsequent Art Deco movement, influenced by both regional and exotic motifs, also counted as modern. Even neoclassical architecture was still pronounced modern into the 1950s and even the 1960s. But Modernism in India was more like an overall approach to life. It meant designing the world positively, improving it, doing better than the required standard, being progressive and inventive, and this certainly included great visionary minds like Tagore and Nehru. British architects in India felt themselves to be modern, because they could work within an experimental field, almost without constraints and regulations, with an unusual degree of freedom. These various trends will now be discussed in a little more detail.

One consequence of the consolidation of British colonial power in the 19th century was that public buildings in particular became the centre of interest. Great educational institutions like Bombay University in 1870 or stations as gateways to the world, like Victoria Station in the former Bombay in 1887, or also important monuments like the Victoria Memorial in Calcutta in 1906, were prestigious structures by a self-confident class of British architects who wanted to demonstrate the superiority of European culture. This was particularly evident when the seat of government moved from Calcutta to Delhi and in 1912 Edwin Lutyens and Herbert Baker were commissioned to realise the government buildings in "New Delhi." The architects designed a monumental urban street complex that was essentially alien to Indian cities, with a grandiose geometry of axes and avenues and above all two symmetrical administrative buildings flanking the view of the viceroy's palace. Lavish colonnades, open verandas, tall, slender windows, *chhajjas* (wide roof overhangs) and cornices *jaalis* (circular stone apertures) and *chhatris* (free-standing pavilions) were used at the same time as decorative elements from typical historic Indian architecture. The viceroy's palace has a dome reminiscent of the Buddhist stupa in Sanchi. Even though Lutyens and Baker fused classical European and Indian elements, the complex seems modern for its day, with its two-dimensional walls, reticent décor and austere geometry in the case of the palace in particular. The seat of government was not opened until 1931, after a building period of almost 20 years. The main neoclassical period lasted well beyond the 1930s, above all because of the influence of the Indian Institute of Architects which existed since the 1920s, a British institution first headed by a Briton, Claude Batley. His theories were based on studies of Graeco-Roman, but also of Indian, classicism. His enormous influence led to the foundation of the conservative school, whose major exponents included Sudlow-Ballardie-Thompson, for example, and Ganesh Deolalikar, who worked up until the 1950s. His Supreme Court in New Delhi imitated the Lutyens-Baker buildings down to the last detail. The conservative, so-called revivalists also included B.R. Manickam with his monumental historical Vidhana Soudha government

Bangalore, Vidhana Soudha ⎯ New Delhi, Garrison Church ⎯ Indian Art Deco house

building in Bangalore built in 1952, reminiscent of Indian palace complexes. Colossal columns, Mogul domes, symmetry and monumental mass were evidence that historical European-Indian forms were being retained. But a new thinking had long since taken hold, based on the reduced formal language of the "international style," but also attached to European abstract Expressionism, as can be seen in Arthur G. Shoesmith's St. Martin's Garrison Church in New Delhi of 1931, whose volumes loom like pure prisms of solid mass thrusting into one another. De Stijl, the important Dutch movement that ran parallel with the Bauhaus, had very little influence on India, however, even though Willem Marinus Dudok did realise some buildings there. In the early 1940s the austerity of what was later called classical Modernism started to be mixed with Expressionism and with decorative motifs, and above all fluent lines, often curved, markedly horizontal and vertical: the highly influential Art Deco movement, which spread over the whole of India, made a triumphant entry into the world of Indian architecture. France, but particularly America, stood model for this movement, whose architects raised Art Deco to an art form of great virtuosity. "Streamlined architecture," as Art Deco was also known, developed its distinctive form partly from the technical achievements of its day, the rounded shapes of aircraft and cars. Then Frank Lloyd Wright discovered the decorative world of the Mexicans and of the Aztecs and Mayans. Their essentially geometrical motifs, along with associated devices like palms, aircraft and sunbeams, finally made their international début on the Art Deco stage. Indian Art Deco was also increasingly mixed with regional applications, leading to some lavishly decorated façades. In an age without television, architects were particularly fond of the generally popular cinema buildings, where they could create Art Deco designs with a monumental gesture. Many of these picture palaces have survived to the present day, providing evidence of a great architectural phase.

At the time of independence in 1947, India had only about 300 trained architects in a population of what was then 330 million, and only one training institution, the Indian Institute of Architects in Bombay. Those who could afford it studied abroad, preferably in the USA, as some Modernist heroes, especially from the Bauhaus, like Mies van der Rohe, Walter Gropius and Marcel Breuer had emigrated to America from Fascist Germany. The first generation of Indian architects came back from America with a new optimism, free of the British influence at the Bombay school, euphoric and able to offer their urgently needed services to a free country. One of them was Habib Rahman, who studied under Gropius at the MIT in Boston, another Achyut Kanvinde from Harvard and Gautam Sarabhai, who worked with Wright in Taliesin. Thus the influence of the Bauhaus masters came to India for a second time, this time directly via their pupils, whose somewhat over-functionalistic interpretations were realised by Kanvinde in particular. But at the same time a new concrete Expressionism was developing in South America, in the work of for example Felix Candela or Oskar Niemeyer, based on the technical possibility of being able to bridge large spans. These impressive constructions stimulated young Indian architects to endow the rigid rationalism of the German teachers in America with fluent form. One of the most important pupils returning from the MIT in Cambridge/Boston in the 1950s was Charles Correa. He had worked under Minoru Yamasaki in Detroit, who later designed the World Trade Center in New York. Correa came back to India in 1958, at a time when the most important architect of the first half of the 20th century, Le Corbusier, had already realised his life's greatest project in India. Le Corbusier was invited by Nehru in person in the early 1950s and built Chandigarh, the new

New Delhi, supreme court — Indian Art Deco house

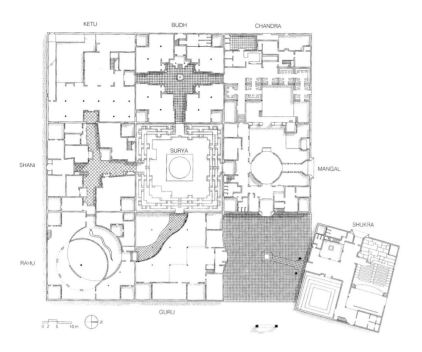

Jaipur, Jawahar Kala Kendra art center

Chandigarh, parliament chamber ⌐ Chandigarh, administrative offices

IIM courtyard complex with library ⌐ Kanchanjunga apartment building

capital of the state of Punjab. Le Corbusier's visionary powers, which he proved in urban developments from the 1920s onwards, seemed to be precisely the right person to Nehru, who said that India needed "a slap in the face." Working with his cousin Pierre Jeanneret and the architects Jane Drew and Maxwell Fry, Le Corbusier realised the entire urban structure, designing himself the government building, the Capitol. His béton brut, the unrendered surfaces of the buildings, still showing the marks of the rough shuttering, and the expressive and sculptural effect made by solitaire monuments spread over a large area, came as something of a shock to the Indian architects, who had found a new hero for themselves from now on.

Le Corbusier's messages became the new gospel for the next generation, who recognised a new intellectual dimension in them. Le Corbusier was commissioned to build more villas and a museum in Ahmedabad. Here he had an Indian at his side who had already worked for him in Paris, Balkrishna Vitaldhas Doshi. It was Doshi who in the early 1960s got in touch with Louis I. Kahn in order to develop the Indian Institute of Management in Ahmedabad. Kahn was impressed by the offer and realised the project during a period of over 13 years. Kahn was the next significant architect for India: his structures built on pure geometry to illustrate inherent order, his turn to a pictorial language for architecture that went beyond functionalism and the use of rough brick for the façade in order to express the nature of the material, added yet another dimension to Indian architects' experience.

Charles Correa developed his work when these two towering 20th century masters were both building in India. His 1963 memorial for Mahatma Gandhi in Ahmedabad, which is reminiscent of Kahn's design for the Trenton Bath House, marks the beginning of his mature work. The most important buildings after that were his Kanchanjunga high-rise apartments in Mumbai, built from 1970–1983, then the government building in Bhopal, 1980–1996 (see p. 26–93), and the art centre in Jaipur, 1986–1992 where he discovered the spiritual dimension of Indian thought and integrated it into his work. Correa is the most important representative of his generation and still India's most significant contemporary architect. Alongside Doshi and Correa, Anant Raje is another major architect of this generation. Raje realised the Indian Institute buildings as Kahn's right hand and added others in the spirit of Kahn. His work is clearly shaped by Kahn's structures, but he interpreted them independently. Raj Rewal also belongs in this group. Educated in Delhi and London, he was influenced at an early stage by the Japanese Metabolists, but later found his own identity in India's history, pursuing the concept of a Modernism based on tradition. His parliament library (see p. 42–49) is one of the outstanding Indian building projects of the last ten years.

The selection of architects from the younger generation introduced here does not claim to be complete or comprehensive within the limited scope of a publication of this kind. Architects who are not mentioned in any more detail here but have certainly made a significant contribution include Laurie Baker in Kerala whose life's work follows economical, ecological and sustainable criteria in building and is devoted above all to people in lower income groups. Similar approaches come from architects like Anil Laul, S.K. Das or the "barefoot architects" in Rajasthan who work together with many people employing their craft skills in the construction process and who use only locally available materials. This book presents a varied spectrum of building types and architects with different approaches to illustrate current trends in Indian architecture, with aspects of ecology and sustainability playing an increasingly important part.

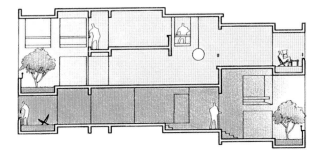

Kanchanjunga apartments, section

1 Amartya Sen, The Argumentative Indian, London 2005, p. 193: "…the ending of poverty and ignorance and disease and inequality of opportunity".
2 Shashi Tharoor, India From Midnight to the Millenium, New Delhi 1997, p. 360.

Buildings (1993 – 2006)

Lower house chamber and exterior wall — Position of the building in town

A building as prominent as the one for the new Vidhan Bhavan in Bhopal in the state of Madhya Pradesh had to take a form imbued with an especially timeless symbolic force transcending functional considerations. Charles Correa and his colleagues actually won the competition in 1980, but building did not start until 1983. After political turmoil, completion of this major building project was delayed until 1997. Realising this extraordinarily remarkable design demonstrated a new self-confidence not just for the individual state and its local government, but for the whole of India, even though Correa had completed his intellectual work on the project long before the phase of economic upswing, India's economic miracle. The new sense of self-awareness was quite obviously present in a design that pulls the whole complex history of the country into focus and conveys it most impressively, in the spirit of the times and yet timelessly, in its realised form.

This can also be measured against the fact that it is very difficult to make a precise estimate of the date the design came into being, as it completely eschews fashionable categories and has lost none of its expressive force, indeed its magic, in 2006, 26 years after it was developed. Correa's synthesis of elements that are deeply rooted in tradition and abstract-modern creative force does, in this intensity, indeed remain a typically Indian or even Asian phenomenony. But it could easily become a model for other cultures: here cultural history is perceived and used in the present as a process of future continuity. Correa's design shows the very presence of history as a respected heritage in India. His design process is still intelligible: not primarily as an analysis of function optimisation generating a form almost of its own accord, but as a prefigurative approach in which the dominant form is worked out first. So following Western linguistic usage, a so-called Postmodern concept was being used here. Assumingly the starting point for the design was the Navgraha Mandala, a square as a symbol of the cosmos, divided into nine additional squares to symbolise seven real and two mythological planets.

This ancient motif, much cited in the pages of this book, is one of the great primal signs of Indian architecture, and has been constantly varied over the centuries to create a spiritual frame of reference. This symbol developed into a preferred sign in Charles Correa's formal vocabulary, one that he used directly and expressively in his design for the cultural centre in Jaipur. But here in Bhopal the Mandala mutated into a fragment: the architect throws an arc of a circle around the square, making the outer corners blunt and incomplete. Thus the circle dominates, as ultimately it forms the outer wall surrounding the building. Within this universe the functional areas are subordinated to the Mandala structure: the great parliamentary chamber for the lower house as another circular figure with foyer; the small chamber for the upper house as a diagonal square; the cabinet area with hall, courtyard and offices; the library; the administrative area with ministerial offices and a large courtyard; a multi-purpose hall; the courtyard for the public and the central hall at the heart of the project. The symmetrical axes are emphasised by three main entrances for the various user groups, but

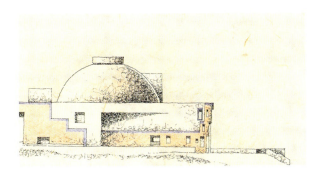

Sketch of the building with lower house chamber

— Charles Correa and Associates
Vidhan Bhavan Government Building
Bhopal (Madhya Pradesh), 1997

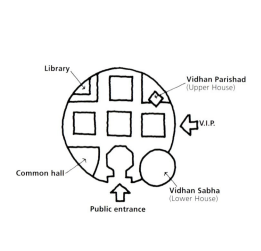
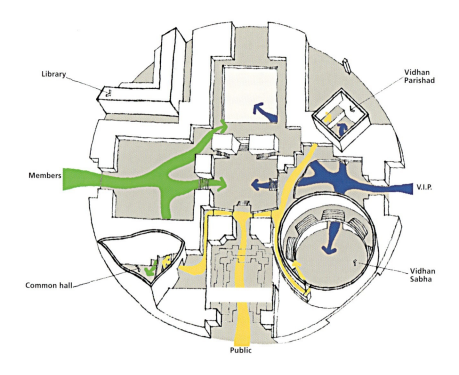

Arrangement of the sub-areas — Access scheme

Sketch of the longitudinal section

also for security precautions. The main entrance for the public is on the south-east side, the VIP entrance on the north side, and the MPs' entrance to the north-west. It becomes clear that Correa is not slavishly bound to the figure of the Mandala, but plays freely around it. The sub-sections are shaped on the basis of their necessary size in such a way that they break through the inherent square structure and in the case of the lower chamber even penetrate the outer wall of the circle. The rigidity of the scheme is broken down, the severe geometry is set in motion and the composition is enlivened by asymmetry. Here the open courtyards providing centres for the sub-areas remain an important ordering motif, calling the structure to mind. They form sub-centres with their own focus, the various departments grouped around them. This concentric aspect of each area shapes the essential function of the courtyard centre as an open or semi-open zone, thus relating directly to the opening above them, to the sky. This gesture clarifies Correa's intention of making the sky and its intense light, its blueness, significant in a way that indicates the above-mentioned spiritual plane. The courtyards also take up an old Indian architectural motif whereby the courtyard provides light and air for the rooms directly in this hot climate, and people are able to spend time outside or inside according to the time of day. The courtyard is also the classical symbol of something shared, a place where people meet, spend time with each other and live together. This aspect is emphasised in the courtyard for the general public, which is placed immediately inside the entrance and constructed in the form of a *Kund*, a large area of stone steps. Here people spend their waiting time together almost as if in a state of communal meditation. A waiting area that would be completely inconceivable in Western culture functions as a "think tank" here, with the ambience of waiting stimulating communal reflection.

Correa's understanding of the timelessness of Indian buildings their enduring validity can be seen particularly well in his concept of alternating open and closed zones and the use of verandas and pergolas, which create a sense of lively space and climate and often become translucent foils for the sky. Creating a microclimate with light and shade and running water leads to a sequence of spaces to be experienced that links the time planes together. When strolling around the government building, the alternating light and air but also the differing levels create a stimulating vibration that reaches its climax in the central area, at the point where all the axes meet. A spiral is inscribed on the floor of the hall at the intersection of all the access routes and a circular aperture cut in the roof; these are motifs that relate to the axis mundi, the axis of the universe. By using the Mandala and the significance of its centre, Correa is alluding to Hindu philosophy, the courtyards as gardens alternating from open to closed are reminiscent of the great Mogul architecture. And one outstanding motif evokes India's Buddhist past: the hemispherical roof of the lower house chamber. It is derived from one of India's great historical monuments, only about 30 km from Bhopal, the Stupa, a stone hemisphere in memory of Buddha, who is said to have spent time meditating there. India's spiritual complexity, expressed in its great diversity today, is woven into this building, thus suggesting that Indian society has always been an amalgam of the greatest possible variety of cultures. But this society held its ground, it allowed itself to be conquered but ultimately absorbed the alien element and made it its own. Hence India's uniqueness and her special position in the world is expressed precisely by the government building in Bhopal, which incorporates the special quality of a country whose anti-imperial, peaceable nature has always led to the absorption of multicultural influences. It also becomes clear how naturally one's own history can be dealt with, and how a virtuosic interpretation of old forms can lead to something new without denying itself. The very position of the government building on a hill in the town is comparable with a citadel, Indian and monumental, a motif from heroic but less peaceful times. And yet it is made clear almost with a twinkle in the eye that the association has been translated playfully. The earthy, brownish quality of the rough external rendering is combined with stone materials and a range from pastel to strong colours from Indian everyday life, decorative bands surround the entrances, artists designed the walls and gates. Correa builds everyday life into his buildings, including people, with their love of colour, variety and abundance. And thus, ultimately, he successfully tied the whole society into his cosmos in a varied and astonishing way, identifying the entire population with this building.

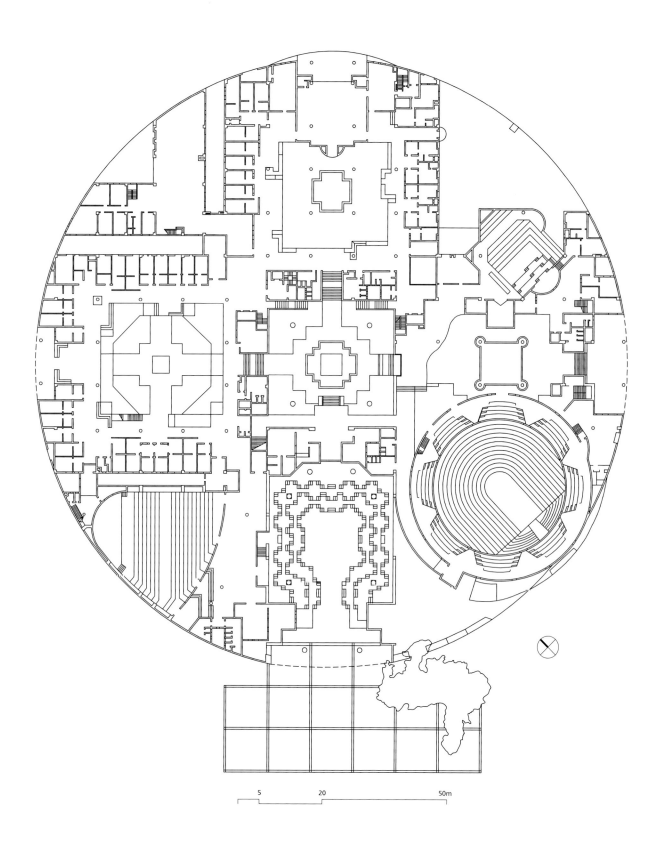

Plan

Vidhan Bhavan Government Building

VIP entrance and lower house chamber — VIP entrance

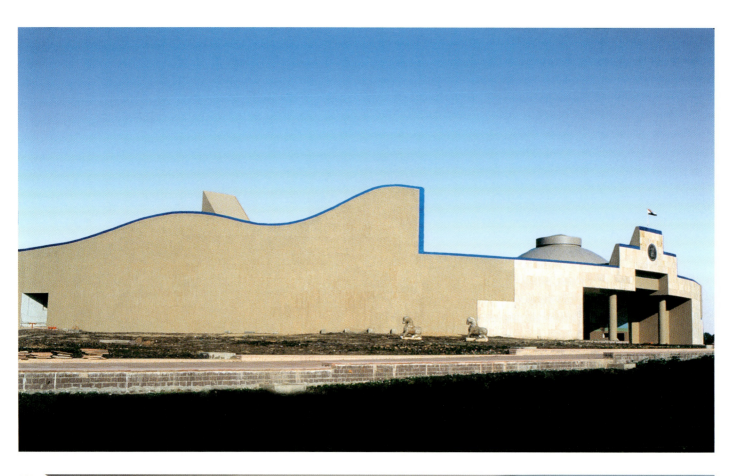

Main entrance for the public and wall of the multi-purpose room — In the public waiting area

The central hall — Entrance to the lower house chamber

Main entrance — The building in the plantation with pavilion

This second home designed by Rahul Mehrotra is in a mango plantation extending approx. 8 hectare, about 5 km north of Ahmedabad. The climate of north-west India is largely dry and hot, so the detached house was placed in the centre of the plantation, so that the evergreen trees can act as a natural filter. Heat and sunlight are greatly mitigated by the all-year-round tree filter, and the direct view into the green shade provides another source of relief. Visitors are intended to experience the house as an introverted stone oasis, protecting, calming, after they have crossed the sea of trees.

The centring theme is continued in the house. A cruciform ground plan places the living-room centrally as a connecting and linking zone. Each arm of the cross acquires a different function: access area with accentuated main entrances and an enclosed courtyard with seating, opposite the dining area with kitchen and ancillary rooms, at right-angles to this the bedroom area for the family and the guest wing on the end. The central residential area opens up into a courtyard with high walls. This means a great deal of extra living space when the large sliding windows are open, as the division consists entirely of glass.

The courtyard is a location for the soul of the house. The area, which is ambivalently placed inside and outside, avoids the stiffness of an unduly rigid cross figure, which would suggest an inappropriate symbolic quality. The centre extends in this simple way, flowing from the roofed, protecting living area into the open outdoor space, and celebrating fundamental elements of our existence: the sphere of the omnipresent blue sky and a narrow pool running along the entire length, clad in blue material. Here the great horizontal of the spatial composition tilts into the vertical: Mehrotra colours the wall that follows the pool of water blue as well, making pool, wall and sky all of a piece. The extension of the water with the blue wall into the living room suggests the concept of living expressed by the courtyard: a spatial connection on the one hand and on the other hand the inclusion of the refreshing and stimulating element in the main area where much time is spent in a hot climate. The very presence of a shimmering pool is enlivening, but the pool also suggests a cooling swim, of course. This "synthesis in blue" becomes the most expressive design element in the house. The architect very deliberately allows the cooling effect of this colour to dominate as a counterpoint to the outside temperature. In this house, colour is not something applied, but entire walls are "plunged into colour," like the red in the corridor leading to the dining area. It becomes an integral part of the architectural sub-figures, and lends them an individual quality, but this does not break the whole composition down. Coloured, smoothly rendered surfaces inside are contrasted with the tactile qualities of natural materials: on the outside the house is clad in sandstone, large wooden doors form independent areas of material, the entrance is a rough exposed concrete frame reminiscent of Le Corbusier, and a stainless steel rain-shield caps the living room window. The extremely carefully balanced scale of materials and colour demonstrates the architect's high degree of sensitivity in an entirely Indian way: strong colour contrasts are derived from

Rahul Mehrotra and Associates
House in a Plantation
Ahmedabad (Gujarat), 2004

Courtyard with pool

an everyday Indian world of magnificent hues, the sandstone, quarried in the vicinity, suggests historical Indian buildings and at the same time reminds of the nearby desert climate. The white of some of the interior plastered walls and materials like exposed concrete and stainless steel are reminiscent of classical-modern design principles. Modern details like profiling, material connections, door furniture and floor coverings show precise workmanship, but above all the intellectual intensity of the architect's handling of his brief.

The interior's openness to the courtyard contrasts with the hermetic quality of the block-like exterior with its identical window slits. Introversion, a classical Indian motif, attempts to create communicative space that will bind the family together in the centre. The courtyard, the patio, the centre open to the sky, appears all over India as part of a domestic culture that is millennia old.

But Mehrotra enriches his building by another dimension: the roof terrace becomes a stone plateau garden, and acquires an exposed concrete pavilion for the cooler evening hours. It is only when looking out over the extensive view of the treetops from the terrace that they become aware of their central location, and the plantation becomes part of the house, a green, organic sea of trees, harmonising with the building's broken autonomy. The strictly consistent geometry of the ground plan figure can be experienced from the roof showing the designer's lucidity and precision, but the timelessness of the building's formal language also expresses its occupants' attitude to life.

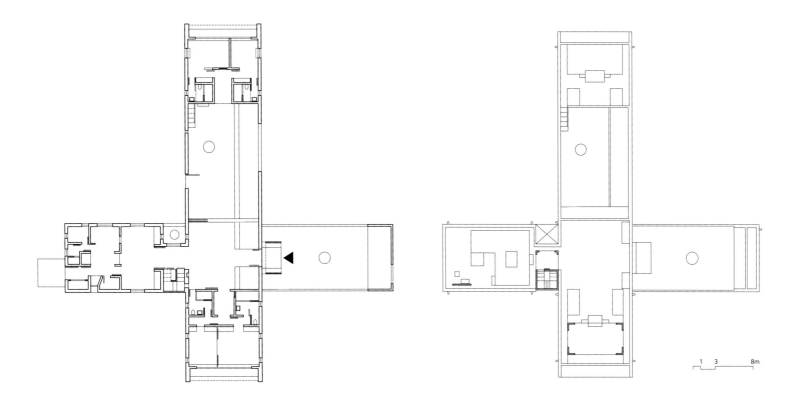

Ground floor plan — Top floor plan

Detail of the wall structures

Courtyard and blue wall

Roof terrace and pavilion ⌐ Roof terrace

View from the courtyard into the living area — View of the main entrance area

Living area and main entrance — Corridor and seating niche

Courtyard with pool — Roof garden with domes and parliament in the background

There was scarcely a more prestigious new building commission put out to tender in India in the last 15 years than the one for a site near the parliamentary buildings from the colonial past. Just like the client, the government, the competition winner, Raj Rewal, was aware of undertaking a historical commission that demanded to be addressed in a way that was up-to-date and could live up to its dominant neighbours. It was essential not to waste the opportunity to present a modern India in this building still aware of its mighty history. The particular difficulty was now to develop an architecture whose credibility hung on a harmonious synthesis of tradition and modernism, that had to be neither historical, nor uncompromisingly modern. The kind of approach that Nehru had intended 50 years ago as a "slap in the face" for India, would not have worked here. Urban development, genius loci and complete respect for the parliament buildings demanded a high degree of subtlety in the treatment of the new building stock. The imperial breath of a not so distant past could still be felt in the place the British architects Edwin Lutyens and Herbert Baker had shaped as New Delhi in the early 20th century with their large-scale planning and impressive buildings. Derived from European cities planned under monarchies, but also influenced by the American design of the capital of Washington, Lutyens and Baker developed geometrical strategies for an urban street plan based on ceremonies and grandeur, the climax presenting the former viceroy's palace, two symmetrical administrative wings and the actual parliament building as a gigantic circle. An important element of the planning was that large areas were to remain free, so that the width and magnificence of the axes should not be impaired.

Lutyens tried to harmonise Western classicism and historical Indian features in his buildings, while Herbert Baker's parliament remained in its structure a purely classical import. An enormous pedestal storey, colossal columns with bases and capitals and a projecting roof level evoke European classical-ancient models. But the building itself, in its sheer size and monumental stereometry turned out to be definitely "modern."

One of the important questions for both the jury and the architect was how to cope with the close proximity to the immense breadth of this colossus. The library site is a triangle adjacent to the parliament, which also has a triangular ground plan, so that it was impossible not to respond to the parliament and indeed to include it in the new plans. Raj Rewal solved this difficult problem magnificently. He did not try to outdo the parliament or confront it with a boastful competitor. He was concerned not to detract from the dominance of the historical and highly esteemed ensemble of buildings, but to retain that dominance, indeed to enhance it if possible in order to create a new weighting. So Rewal transfers the parliament's monumental gesture only in the form of a strictly axial quality running through both centre points and creating the first main link. He further chooses the square as a basic geometry, which equals the circle as an archaic element, and also contains its concentricity, with the diagonal of the library square corresponding to the diameter of the parliament's circle. The figures of both buildings draw

Roof garden

—Raj Rewal and Associates
Indian Parliament Library
New Delhi (Delhi), 2003

Entrance hall — Detail of the dome structure in the entrance hall — Centre hall with glass dome

life from this centre, where the most important things happen. The architect shows self-confidence by choosing a geometrical figure with a double axis allowing the new building to assert itself emphatically vis-à-vis its neighbour. But one quality in particular concerns him that the parliament does not have, and that is the typological feature of a typically Indian continuity.

In contrast with the mass of the parliament as a unit and an entirety, illustrated in the building's exterior by the infinite curve of the circle, the mass of the library is a multiple, consisting of curved individual building sections, but tied together in a rigidly fixed ordering structure. The parts of the library are assembled like satellites around an interior that is also structured. By choosing this motif of an "active" concentricity, by allowing exterior and interior to communicate like this, Rewal is trying to derive his design directly from the historical context of India's most important buildings. Millennia-old Hindu temples vary this motif in a multitude of ways, Mogul architecture like the Taj Mahal, the city of Jaipur in north Rajasthan or also the ideal cities in south India are all based on this concentric structure. The form is seen as a spiritual motif alluding to a cosmological dimension, a "cosmogram." Largely divided into nine parts which indicate seven existing and one imaginary planet of the solar ecliptic, the centre as the *axis mundi*, the axis of the universe, the source of all creation. Architecture as an image of the cosmos is a primeval motif of Indian building, and is interpreted here in a new context as a "house of growing knowledge." This is a simple but highly abstract motif, and with its pure geometry it contains a timeless dimension. Yet its very real differentiation also suggests the complexity of the secular element of the building commission. In this way the library design emancipates itself completely from the predominance of the parliament and retains its own identity.

One external dimensional aspect in particular underlines this intention: Rewal does not allow his building to rise any higher than the base floor of the parliament, it retains a pointedly humble horizontal quality, with only the internal roof superstructures attaining any greater height. Two additional storeys are buried underground, thus creating a low, pavilion-like group of buildings. With this basic concept, the architect achieves a successfully subtle solution to the parliament building and the need to integrate his work into the prominent urban structure. The main entrance is thus placed on the parliament side, and its hall leads visitors and users into the centre or the wings that form the ring. The administrative section is placed on the outside, and departmental functions like press centre, digital library and large auditorium are at the nodal points. The centre is made up of the parliamentarians' reading room, research area and archive, and the committee room. But the junction point in the centre remains empty, the axis mundi becomes a multi-storey hall, with a glass dome and flooded with light as it is the only hall, symbolising growing knowledge and consciousness to the point of "enlightenment." Because of the presence of an existing grove of trees, one corner of the powerfully symbolic square remains empty, the essentially rigid and austere figure of the library is broken up and changes into an

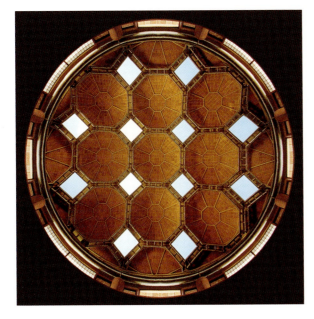 

Dome structure with skylights in the entrance hall — Model of the parliament library

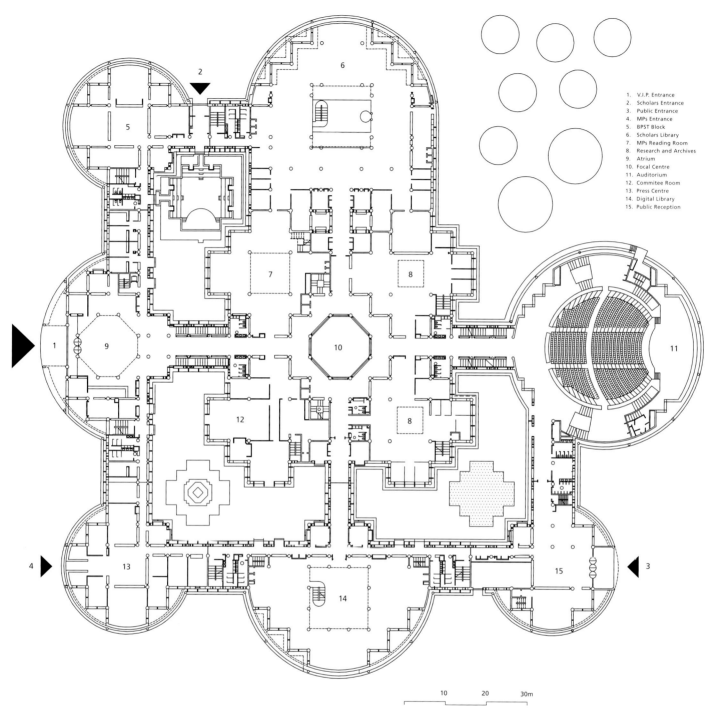

Ground floor

asymmetrical, incomplete fractal geometry. Here Rewal is following an entirely modern structural idea of axiality, symmetry and the disturbance of symmetry as a component of our thinking today. The whole that is entirely complete as such, absolute and fixed, in equilibrium, does not exist as an ideal, the break suggests change, development, growth, it symbolises the relative and includes the unpredictable. Courtyards are created between centre and ring, also a classically Indian motif from a hot climate, offering protection from heat, dust and noise, but also making spiritualisation and concentration possible. This produces charged, changing spatial sequences as one moves through the building: halls as centres of sectional areas with vertical connections, corridors with adjacent horizontal outer spaces that open up, and introverted zones for reading and work.

Rewal's choice of materials for his wall claddings emphasises come close to the atmospheric quality of a historic spatial sequence: all the façades are covered with red and beige sandstone, left rough outside and polished inside. Of course this seems like a reference to the building's neighbour, as the parliament is also built in this particular stone combination, but the link with Indian history is more in the forefront of Rewal's mind. He contrasts massive piers with slender columns, articulates the exterior walls with a decorative structure and grades the building in transitions from circle to square to create deep areas of shadow. And yet concrete and other modern materials remain visible everywhere, and the honesty of the structure adds to its enduring presence. But the architect goes further, stepping up his structural design elements in an unusual way. The halls at the junction points inside the structure and the special spaces like the great reading rooms, the central research and archive areas, but also the cafeteria, are given dome structures made of prefabricated lightweight concrete segments fitted together in a hexagonal and octagonal honeycomb structure. Rewal braces these domes with tubular steel systems that are also hexagonal and octagonal, acting as a substructure. The forces are dispersed via enormous tubular circles on piers. Here the architect employs classical Indian elements from Mogul architecture in particular, as domes were important features of Muslim rulers' buildings. These great models are quoted in the hatlike protrusions of these domes, but above all in the almost full openings in the circular hearing zones which indirectly control the light. Thus light is admitted to the space below the dome, which is then reflected by the dome as a kind of light trap, and the dome itself is placed "in the right light." But Rewal emphasises the interpretative character by his choice of construction method, thus wishing to see the historical model transported into our day. It is only the steel connections of contemporary technology that make this multiform material symbiosis possible. At the same time they evoke European models that Rewal must have got to know on his working visit to France, Henry Labrouste and Viollet-le-Duc.

Seen from the Western European point of view, the new library building for the Indian parliament perhaps slightly overemphasises the classical-historical interpretation. But for Indians the library seems to have the right expressive quality at the right point. Its form symbolises an implicit and diverse democracy, integrating the spiritual dimension that is rooted so deeply in the Indian soul and thus showing the neighbouring government buildings from a different era in a new light: the government quarter has become truly Indian.

Centre hall with glass dome — Glass dome in evening light

Interior railing detail

Glass dome — Window in the office area

View of the entrance

REGIONALISTIC-MODERN

Shimul Javeri Kadri Architects (SJK) had set themselves a particular challenge with this building commission for a textile processing company: paying very close attention to the genius loci, the spirit of the place. The all-female team did not intend to construct a normal industrial plant, but to develop a building that reflects this local character, while at the same time interpreting it. The building was to fit in without attempting to ingratiate itself, do justice to scale, but assert itself in every detail, pick up elements of the existing buildings but offer solutions of its own. In the largely hot and dry climate, a humane and social atmosphere was to go hand in hand with local technology and materials available in the immediate vicinity. This not only helped to keep the costs down, but also gave local people the opportunity to be actively involved in the construction process. In this way the local workforce would be able to accumulate experience in handling the materials and later identify with this new "product" they had made themselves, a by no means unimportant factor in a rural area. The architects started to study the place and established that the anonymous buildings had many kinds of large and small courtyards, striking gable walls on a lot of the houses featured doors and windows crafted in the local carpentry tradition. A long-established skill in making metal door and window furnishings was in evidence, and a large quarry was available. These factors became criteria for their own design. As Shimul Kadri said, the human aspect of space should play a major part. Thus the courtyards, where the women prepared food in a variety of ways and ran the households, with animals sitting there to keep them company, expressed on architecture for everyday life. Similarly, space in the new production building is stimulating and inspiring, its scale, materials and the way it links with other spaces relates clearly to the locality and above all it allows for pleasant temperatures, in other words, it shows "hygiene" (Shimul Kadri). The functions of parking for delivery vehicles, unloading, handling, packing and loading were to be fitted into a polygonal, sloping site in such a way that everything ran as smoothly as possible, and so that there was no possibility that the buildings should fall into disrepair and thus introduce random and heterogeneous elements. The team of architects designed a building that contains everything on one level, where the different functions are not separated but brought together "in a single stream."

Because the terrain slopes, the building has a large base, a platform on which all the sub-areas are assembled. The entrance is at the southern tip of the plot. It is emphasised by a curved wall, and its traditional wooden door invites people to enter. From there a corridor leads through the entire centre of the complex as a kind of spine. The production rooms are arranged in a line down one side, while the open gallery on the other side opens first to a small inner courtyard, then comes a large courtyard space and green area, and finally the gallery runs into the open, but roofed cafeteria with kitchens and sanitary area attached. The functional difference between the two sides is also expressed in the outside lines of the building: the production is linear, with angles, while the courtyard side describes a gentle curve. A surprising material was chosen as a shell for the entire external

—Shimul Javeri Kadri Architects
Production Building for Synergy Lifestyles
Karur (Tamil Nadu), 2004

Main entrance — View of the entrance through the gate

envelope: rough quarrystone masonry in granite, which is usually chosen only for foundations. The stone comes from the local quarry, thus expressing the link with the locality. Cost comparisons between the usual rendered masonry and quarrystone showed that both come out about the same, so the long-lasting granite, which needs no maintenance, was chosen. The trained local workforce was well qualified to build with it. The rough character of the stone which could have been forbidding, is combined with warm wooden doors and windows and contrasted with the interior, which is rendered in light-coloured plaster throughout. The traditional front door with its striking craftsmanship gives a foretaste of the interior architecture, which impressively combines the clear lines and smooth surfaces required by modern taste with traditionally crafted wooden windows and metal door and window furnishings made on the basis of old processes. The floor materials, red terracotta alternating with black Cuddapah stone, and the wooden benches and tables in the cafeteria also draw on customary items from the everyday world of the surrounding area. The little inner courtyard near the entrance and the large courtyard in the centre interpret the courtyard architecture of the local buildings. They make it possible to light the adjacent rooms indirectly, which is important, and their pools help to make them into little oases for relaxing between work sessions. Light and temperature control are important aspects of these courtyards, but they are just as much places to meet and communicate. Courtyards are always windy places, and air can be vented into the surrounding rooms as needed. The gables on houses are another important local feature that the architects carry over into their work. Here they are put to lavish architectural use: they are tied together in additive series via an even curve, like a wave pattern. They hide the half-barrel vaults for the production halls, which account for the curve. But there is no doubt that this wave was also deliberately intended to alienate the usual house gable, as it is part of the concept for a design shaped by discreet rounding and curvature. The half-barrels are oriented east-west, so that anti-dazzle skylights allow northern and southern light into the rooms; such light has an even quality so near the equator.

Steering clear of the usual industrial container Shimul Javeri Kadri and her colleagues have achieved their aim. They developed a building that looks modest and yet is self-confident and unusual, and its "feel-good atmosphere" certainly helps to motivate the employees. Its scale, the careful detailing and consideration for local conditions, even in the production area, make it stand out conspicuously from the usual monotony of functional buildings. The combination of regional and traditional elements with the global aspects of its owners' and operators' export activity is reflected in the building – an example for a credible contemporary architectural language developed from tradition.

Entrance door

Production Building for Synergy Lifestyles

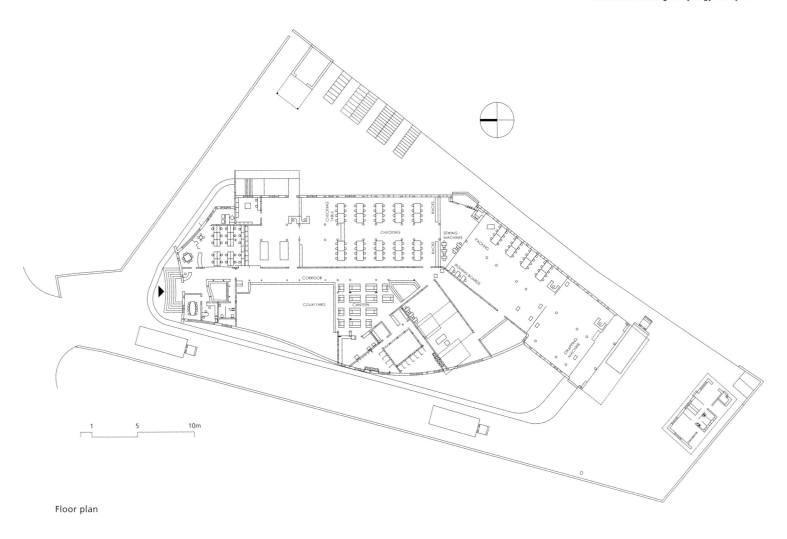

Floor plan

Raising the rubblestone walls

The production area from the rear

View of the outer boundary wall with courtyard — The loading zone

Production Building for Synergy Lifestyles

Rear façade of the halls

Corridor at the cafeteria — Light well at the entrance

Production Building for Synergy Lifestyles

The large courtyard with pool

The production halls — Window detail

59

On a dormitory gallery — The open courtyard in the Kahn building

A great weight of responsibility fell on the shoulders of Bimal Patel and his practice with its long abbreviation HCP-DPM, when they won the competition to extend the Indian Institute of Management (IIM) in Ahmedabad. Adding to one of the great monuments of late modern architecture with a world-wide reputation needed not just a precise analysis of the existing building, but also the greatest possible ability to empathise in terms of the dialogue between the two building complexes that was necessarily initiated. The IIM project was realised by Louis I. Kahn from 1962 to 1974 and continued after his death by Anant Raje. It was designed and built as an entity, as something complete in itself. It also included the Management Development Center (MDC) buildings, designed by Raje in Kahn's language and based on a concept of Kahn, and an auditorium with administration wing immediately adjacent to the Kahn buildings. 30 years ago there was no intention to extend the buildings on a large scale, so Kahn developed the plan of a hierarchically staggered ensemble of the entire site. The library dominated at the head of the school complex, then came the lecture theatres and the office wing, followed by the diagonal structure of the students' accommodation and finally the other residential buildings. Hence it was not possible to realise an extension on this original campus site, which was completely covered with a sophisticated residential building structure for employees as well as the school buildings and the student accommodation. So ultimately it was decided to use an adjacent plot, even though it was separated off by a busy road. Patel and his colleagues tried to forge a link: the site of the new complex was to be directly accessible via an underpass. It is now possible to access the new campus quite safely from an existing path leading between the lecture theatres and dormitories and along the separate canteen building in the old complex. Thus the first hurdle in dealing with the existing building stock was overcome by this gesture of maintaining a respectful distance from the Kahn building, which is highly esteemed both for its world-famous architecture but also as an educational institution. The Kahn building remained untouched, yet the incompleteness of the original design, as shown in the opening courtyard, was taken as an invitation to realise the new complex so that it could address this opening. Thus the courtyard, the "Louis Kahn Plaza," at the end of which Kahn himself had intended to place the kitchen and canteen as a link between the wings, acquires a new level of meaning: the opening points towards the new buildings and suggests a connection.

The following functional areas were to be accommodated in the new building complex: teaching rooms for the Post-Graduate Programme (PGP) with five lecture theatres, seminar rooms and offices, then nine halls of residence for 340 students and 20 buildings for married students; then for the MDC four lecture halls, seminar rooms, a refectory and 160 apartments, and finally sports facilities and a water-tower. Kahn's successful idea of making learning and living into an entity was also pursued by Patel and his colleagues. Their difficult challenge was to develop an independent architecture that would still carry and interpret traces and structures from Kahn's building. In a kind of mirror image the dominant

The Kahn building before the extension

— HCP Design and Project Management Pvt. Ltd.
Indian Institute of Management New Campus (IIM)
Ahmedabad (Gujarat), 2006

View of the dormitories from the lecture rooms

View of the lecture rooms from the garden courtyards — View of the lecture rooms from the dormitories

form of the dormitories from the old complex is taken up and used as a means of structuring the new functional areas. Lecture halls on the axis of the old classrooms are arranged as a "backbone" and guiding line, with the MDC and all the areas attached to it added at right angles on the north side. The student dormitories are arranged on a diagonal opposite the lecture hall axis, as individual halls of residence, similarly to the Kahn concept, but this time facing west. Residential units with detached houses for married students are placed on the west side of the plot, in a staggered structure. Kahn's living and learning buildings are far more closely linked, they really do form a unit, not least because brick is universally employed as a completely homogenising material. This "all of a piece" approach was abandoned as well as the close linkage in terms of proximity. Patel's buildings are more like an urban complex, some standing close together and some further apart, with city-style squares and a large axis ending in the water tower. The residential units are larger, contain more students, are further apart, certainly for reasons of economy as well. The intimate quality of Kahn's architecture with its buildings snuggling close together, with shadier courtyards, sudden changes of level and little flights of steps and arcades, are abandoned in favour of a generous spacious quality on the same level. Even the common room inside the dormitories, seen as a particularly meaningful central area for student communication by Kahn, is shifted on to the periphery of the buildings. Perhaps present-day students' need for more seclusion and concentration are the reasons for these changes. But the new dormitories are more comfortable, larger, and have lifts and individual bathrooms, an absolute luxury for occupants of the old complex. Probably the material chosen marks the greatest difference between the old and the new campus. Patel and his colleagues thoroughly discussed the question of whether they should continue to use Kahn's material, whether the homogeneity of the whole, i.e. of both complexes, had to be a criterion. They came to the conclusion that the newness of the buildings should also be expressed in the materials, as the new campus was to embody a new age and the "modernisation of India as a whole" (Patel). This credo acquired symbolic material form in exposed concrete, smoothly shuttered and carefully worked, not the rough *béton brut* used by an architect like Le Corbusier in Chandigarh. But this material also refers subtly to the other master, as Kahn is considered to have invented concrete with a smooth surface, precisely pressed into steel shuttering. His 1959 Salk Institute in San Diego signposted this way of working with the material, and is still exemplary. It also acted as a stimulus for another master builder, Tadao Ando, who made it his trademark. Here the smooth concrete ties all the buildings together. It is combined with narrow brick panels for the dormitories and wears very well in contrast to the brick used for the Kahn buildings, which does not resist heat so well. Little details like walls placed diagonally, round apertures and semi-circular staircase towers are also reminiscent of the old buildings, without degenerating into kitsch. With the fundamental formal analogies of a rigid geometry, the simplicity and reticence of the architectural language, paired with the austerity of large, even walls, pays tribute to the master, but without copying him. Bimal Patel hopes to have done Kahn an honour in creating an architecture in his spirit where students are educated to think critically and attentively, just as Kahn once intended.

The lecture room line-up

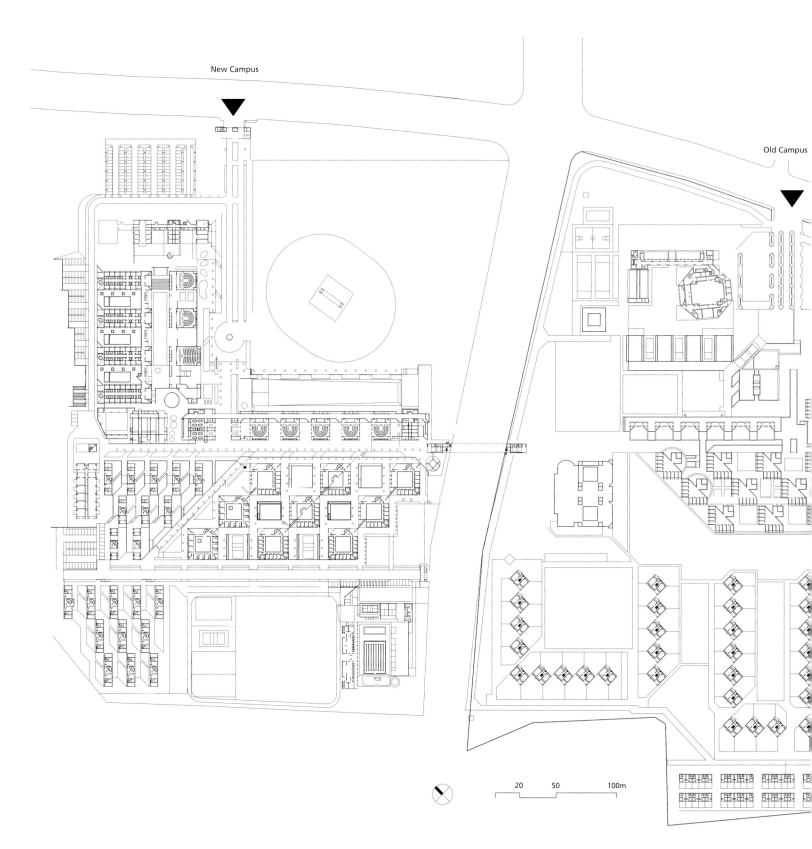

Site plan

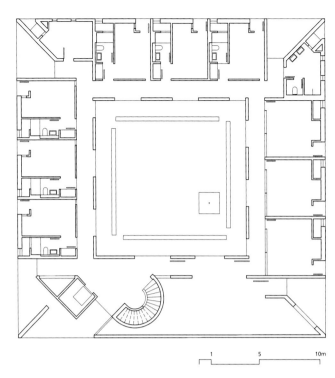

Dormitory, ground floor

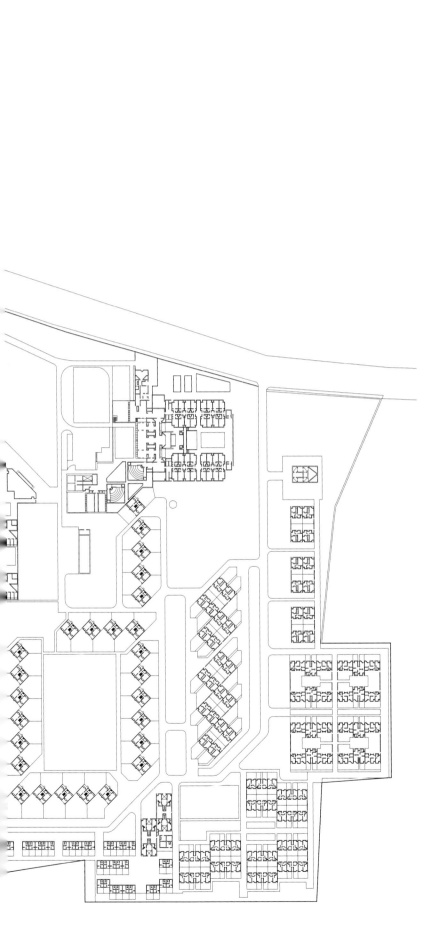

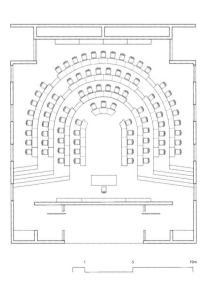

Lecture room

Dormitories and the area surrounding them — Garden courtyards between the dormitories

Inner courtyard of a dormitory — Lecture room

Indian Institute of Management New Campus

Dormitory with diagonal access — Corridor with light wells

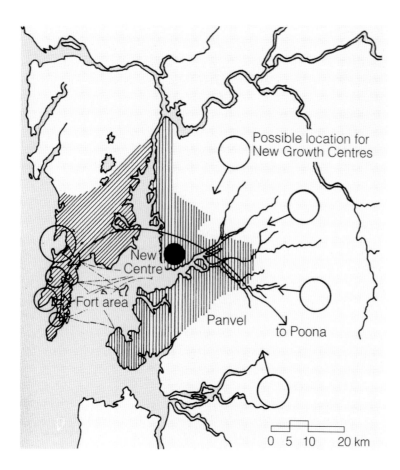

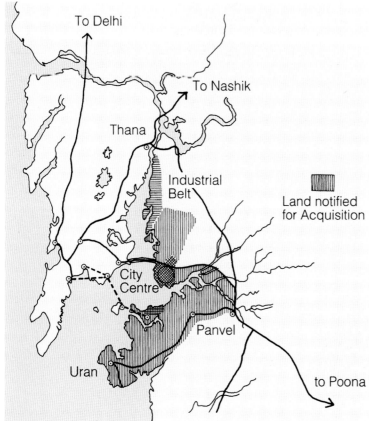

Old and New Mumbai — New Mumbai

Planning for New Mumbai Mumbai, formerly Bombay, is the commercial and financial centre of India, with a population of about twelve million at the time of writing. The huge city is growing by many thousand hopeful immigrants from predominantly rural areas each day. Mumbai's particular topography – it is a long, narrow peninsula – meant that the constantly needed extension of the city limits was possible in one direction only, northwards. Britain's efforts as a colonial power 200 years ago were directed at „citifying" something that was essentially a withdrawn little town because of its outstanding location as a harbour and trading centre. But Bombay did not start to flourish until 50 years later, when the turmoil of the Civil War cut off American cotton export. So the world focused its interest on Indian cotton, and Bombay became the centre for the shipment of goods. Ultra-fast growth began, the port became the largest in India, and rapid urban expansion created the problem of a housing shortage and a proliferation of emergency accommodation. The centre of Mumbai, now and then, is at the southern end of the peninsula, where commercial life developed and population density and land prices are highest. The extreme expansion of the urban area to one side of a fixed commercial centre created Mumbai's major problems of long transport routes. Journeys lasting several hours on express trains had to be accepted if people were to get to work, a state of affairs that eventually reached its natural limits.

As early as 1964, Charles Correa with his colleagues Pravina Mehta and Shiresh Patel proposed to the Mumbai city authorities that they should not expand any further northwards, but use an eastern site cut off by a sea bay for urban expansion, with the aim of establishing New Mumbai. The government did not finally accept this plan until 1970, when it started to buy land east of Mumbai old town. Large bridges then made it possible to create a direct link with the old centre, so that there was now nothing else in the way of the actual goal of a new commercial centre with a new urban structure. The City and Industrial Development Corporation (CIDCO) was founded, and Charles Correa headed it as chief architect from 1970 to 1974. Their aim was to settle at least four million people in New Mumbai, thus containing the spread of further emergency accommodation and creating enough new jobs. There were two key aspects to be dealt with: creating living space and setting up mass transport systems. The southern sub-centre called Ulwe, for which Correa produced a development plan, is now part of New Mumbai. The intention was to carry out real town planning here, with the colonial British planning in Old Mumbai definitely providing a model: a development and use plan was drawn up in co-operation with CIDCO, rules were fixed, i.e. the building development structures, building heights and street width etc., and a start made by designing 1000 dwellings for 350,000 inhabitants. Every income group was to be considered here, and cost/use factors devised in categories, for example clay or bamboo buildings for lower income groups, masonry buildings for middle income groups and apartments for high earners. The complexity of a city as an urban organism meant that flexibility had to be a factor as well, with room for natural growth. Urban quality in the sense of an ambience appropriate to human scale meant considering factors like varied living space dependent on urban density, structures

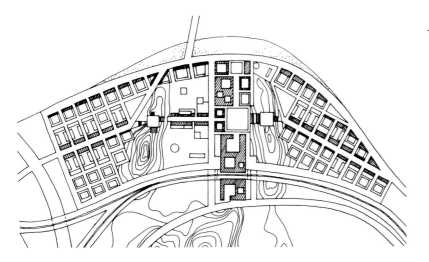

Charles Correa and Associates
Town Planning in Mumbai and Bagalkot
Mumbai (Maharashtra), Bagalkot (Karnataka)
under construction

The development plan for the centre of Ulwe

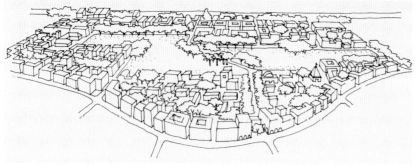

The structure of Ulwe — The development structure of Ulwe

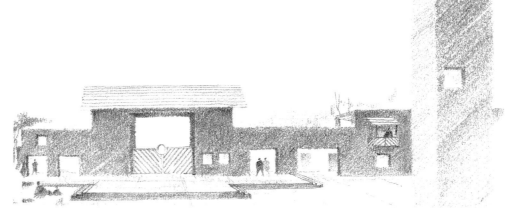

The centre of Ulwe

like neighbourhoods and quarters, public buildings and areas, also sufficient green areas and open spaces, and transport with adequate stopping points. Correa developed a complex and flexible urban structure for Ulwe, but at the same time laid down strict building guidelines to guard against Indian urban sprawl: urban blocks as the basic structure, with fixed building height, numbers of floors and street and rear façades, and also fixed use dependent on position within the city. An urban centre offered administration, public buildings, green areas and transport links with buses and trains. This ambitious, fixed structure – and thus inimical to the Indian free spirit – has been under construction for several decades.

Planning for New Bagalkot New dams caused the Ghataprabha River in the state of Karnataka to rise and flood parts of the old town in Bagalkot. A new centre, New Bagalkot, was proposed and planned to accommodate 100,000 people. Charles Correa was faced with similar problems as in Ulwe, just on a smaller scale, but even greater flexibility was needed for the building development and the street space. Here what were called „planned-unplanned" elements had to be factored in, as a great deal was to be left to the people themselves. As natural growth was seen to be desirable, it was important to lay down rough urban development guidelines only. These addressed the size of the quarters, linked routes through the town, the transport systems and stopping points, and not least, the building development structure. Correa prescribed a hierarchical geometrical structure that resembles the diagram of the Mandala, the old Hindu symbol of the cosmos. Indian town planning has been linked to the abstract idea of the cosmos for centuries, an idea that Correa takes up here.

A square, consisting of seven times seven quarter zones, is oriented precisely according to the points of the compass, and is broken down into green areas running right on into the centre along its diagonals, but also along its orthogonal lines. Here a pool of water framed by stone steps, a *Kund*, acquires the symbolic importance of the axis mundi, the world axis of the universe. The centre was developed strictly in blocks, grouped around the pool of water in the prescribed geometrical fashion. The design that Correa prescribed for the building development inside the quarters is very dense in the centre and slowly but surely decreasing in density towards the edges of the quarters, with the possibility of breaking up altogether. Only a few dominant street links are laid down, so that connecting routes can emerge by their own accord during the growth period. Different housing types were to meet the needs of all income groups, with relatively high density development packed tightly into the quarter as a whole, was intended to create the typical oriental bazaar atmosphere. This design, which applies metaphysical symbolism to historical models in particular, has also been under construction since 1985.

Anonymous buildings with residents

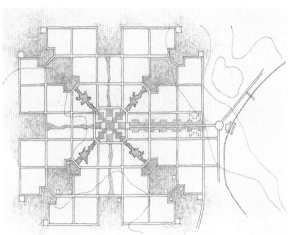 

Diagram of New Bagalkot — Old Bagalkot

Centre of New Bagalkot

Town Planning in Mumbai and Bagalkot

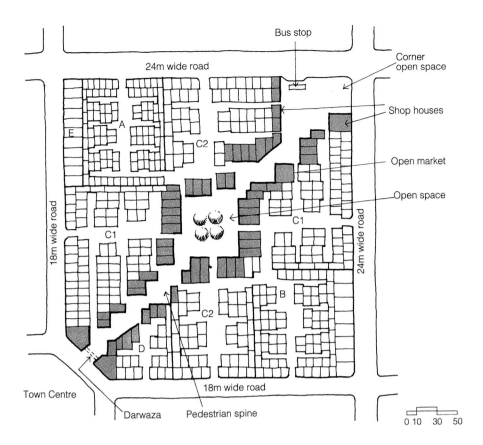

Quarter development

View of the development

View of the whole complex — Multi-storey buildings with roof terraces

This building project by the City and Industrial Development Corporation (CIDCO) by Maharashtra state represents a complex, specifically Indian problem: creating accommodation for people on subsistence incomes. Fundamentally, these are homes that can never be owned by their occupants, because in most cases the people who live there will never succeed in breaking through the income barriers. People usually get stuck within a social stratum that is clearly defined and demarcated without any hope or chance of improvement because of inadequate schooling and professional training. Other factors, too, play a part in the Hindu social system, especially the caste system, a millennia-old structure into which one is born. Over the centuries, a system that ordered and stabilised society into professional classes degenerated into an unworthy class system that despises human beings. Despite the Indian government's best efforts to break away from it, sometimes using force, and to guarantee better chances of success for those involved, this scourge still remains firmly anchored in people's consciousness.

Raj Rewal's practice was commissioned to plan 1000 accommodation units for residents on the edge of a large planning area in New Mumbai, a new area that was being developed at the time east of Mumbai old town. As is the case with all urban development projects, despite a very low budget it was important not just to provide the bare essentials in terms of space, but above all to develop a home environment that was simple but of high quality. The difficult balancing act between finance and ambience could succeed only if inexpensive but lastingly effective building materials were used, and if the planning process was not too costly and led a simple implementation procedure. The Rewal practice designed the project as a high density structure. On the one hand it was because the area available was strictly limited, but also in order to achieve quality for the outdoor space that was effective in urban terms, yet reminiscent of a naturally developed village. These accommodations cells, or "molecules" (Rewal), now consist of one to three room units 18, 25, 40 and 70 m² large. They have essential sanitary facilities and water tanks on the roof for a constant water supply, which is still by no means to be taken for granted in essentially rural India.

One important problem had to be solved: what reasonably priced and durable materials could make a lasting effect within a very tight financial framework. The final choice was a combination of concrete cavity blocks, exposed plasterwork, hand-made terracotta tiles and locally available rough granite stones for the base. This combination can endure the hard monsoon climate and will develop an acceptable patina. Electricity was also guaranteed for the entire complex, not just in the dwellings themselves, but in the public areas as well. Roads were moved to the periphery to allow for safe but reasonably priced footpath connections within the development. There is access on all sides from the outside, and it is easy for people to filter through the building groups. With the concept of a very dense residential quarter, Rewal accomodated the enormously high level of social interaction in everyday Indian life. People do not just live in their own homes, but are in intensive contact with neighbours, friends

―Raj Rewal and Associates
CIDCO Lowcost Housing
New Mumbai (Maharashtra), 1993

Car-free internal access

and fellow occupants almost throughout the day and night. Thus opening the homes up to the outdoor space is an important design consideration. Increased urban density is now not usually born of necessity, but an important concept for life in general. When developing urban space the quality of indoor and outdoor space have to go hand in hand, as life takes place to a large extent in the street. So when planning the chain of "molecules", great emphasis was laid on the connections implied by communally used spaces. In India, a "village" consists of an accumulation of squares, courtyards, loggias, terraces and balconies where people communicate and make the exchanges that are so essential to life. Rewal considers these factors on a large scale and builds these zones into his architecture. He develops a type of building kit system with cubic basic elements. These admit a wide range of highly flexible variation as a design principle and can thus be used almost universally: courtyards turn individual blocks into chains, modules are set very close together, blocks with courtyards are grouped as quarters. This shows a theme being kept consistently and implemented with great virtuosity. Efficiency is not the only key factor, it is important to create a living environment on the basis of a wealth of space. A structure emerges that is completely homogeneous not just as a physical entity, but also in terms of its materials, a design that is all of a piece, and yet at the same time a highly sophisticated residential unit with complex spatial diversity. The fact that the buildings all have different numbers of storeys contributes to this, being staggered from one to four levels, and so does the slope on the site. A sloping site dynamises and extends the space and the physical quality of the buildings and enhances the image of a living organism that seems as though it could be extended at any time. The totality of the planning is expressed in homogeneity, emphasising the holistic design. There is no attempt to duplicate the individual dwellings artificially, no false sense of growth, which gives the architectural approach its complete credibility. Rewal is very consistently demonstrating a concept that has nothing nostalgic about it in terms of overall appearance: reduction was essential, and from this necessity is born an abstract and thus unambiguously modern form, entirely committed to its time.

Two models of the structure of a quarter

Site plan

Courtyards and terraces

CIDCO Lowcost Housing

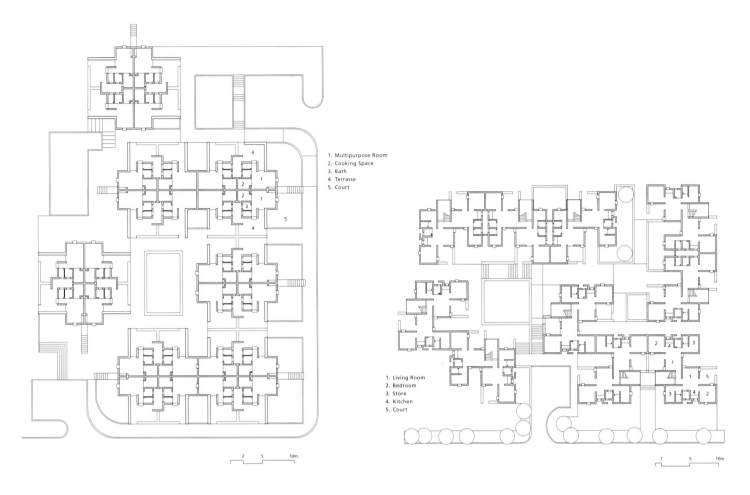

Building group 1 — Building group 2

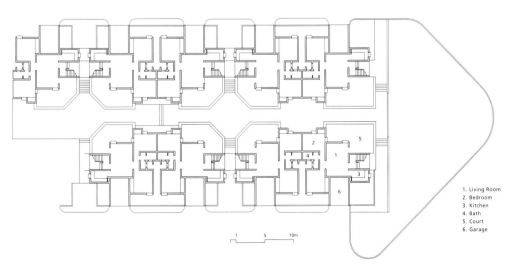

Building group 3

View of roofs and terraces — Façade detail

Roofed courtyards ⎯ Between the buildings

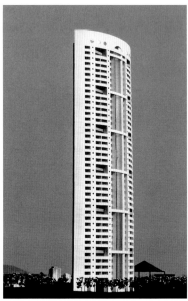

Tytan apartment block — Belvedere apartment block

The Khareghat and Associates practice describes its own work as International Style, trying in this way to link up with the stylistic period of Modernism that is generally also called "classical." But from an Indian point of view this international concept is ambiguous: it is not just retrospective, relating to a past architectural epoch, but also prospective in the sense of looking forward, to emphasise India's own international qualities. "International" is a new key word in the Indian consciousness and is used wherever possible to underline the country's changed economic situation and the new ways in which its people think.

Khareghat have made a name for themselves in the last ten years with high-rise buildings which in contrast to most buildings, especially in the Greater Mumbai area, make an impact through their austerity. Behind this is a design approach that borrows from classical Modernism by particularly emphasising reduced, if not to say abstract form. This approach is being continued with two residential tower blocks that are under construction in central Mumbai. The 30 to 40 storey buildings are going up on expensive plots. They will be among the highest in the whole of India and offer a breathtaking panorama of the city and the entire coastline. This is why one of them will be called Belvedere. It will contain three- and four-bedroom apartments in over 40 storeys, and every six floors there will be an apartment on two levels. There are two apartments per storey each with a main entrance and a side entrance leading directly into the kitchen, an important functional aspect in an Indian household. A guest area is placed near the main entrance, while the family rooms are in the back. Living room and master bedroom are glazed on two sides, allowing through draught into the rooms, which is of high importance in the largely hot metropolitan climate of India. The building stands on a podium, an entrance plateau that accommodates an underground car park in the basement. An open but pyramidal roofed swimming pool is seen as a piece of architectural counterpoint and is available for residents' use.

The form of the building derives from its situation and the associated orientation: an arc on the side with the view of the coast creates a clear front and back for the building. At the rear – and set well away from the main building – is a rectangular block divided in two by central steps describing a segment of a circle. The rear block alludes to the clear orthogonal structure of the interior, and the rear steps and an incision in the main façade to the symmetry and structure of the ground plan. One of the Khareghat practice's design principles is overlaying primary geometry with the strictly rectangular ground plan structure. But this means that one element finds its way into the design that relativises the classical-modern approach: prefiguration. The volume of the cylinder segment with a block set back behind is based on a prefigurative approach in which the circle is thought of first, and then followed by the function programme that matches it. To Western minds this is the voice of Postmodernism, in other words the phase of a defeated Modernism that prescribes form and is no longer developed purely from function, as proclaimed by the architecture of the 1920s and 1930s. Yet the lucid building section with its light colours and even

—Khareghat and Associates
Belvedere and Tytan Apartment Blocks
Mumbai (Maharashtra), under construction

Belvedere apartment block, side view — Rear view

"window perforation" corresponding with the internal function does cite functionalistic Modernism. The rhythm and dimensions of the balcony and window apertures were carefully adjusted to match the overall volume, and the façades are not dominated by autonomous formalism. Discipline maintains the upper hand.

This formal thinking is intensified in a second design for an apartment block under construction in Mumbai. The tower is called Tytan, and also offers spectacular views of the city and the sea. In this case all the apartments have four bedrooms, with one apartment per floor in the 32-storey building and penthouses on the top of three double floors. The prefigurative approach is immediately recognisable, as the orthogonal structure of the ground plan is "disturbed" by a surrounding diagonal square. Symmetry is developed across the diagonal, than cancelled again on one side of the steps. Even though the ground plan suggests a hierarchical structure, the diagonal placing avoids a clear front and back. Here the architect himself stated that he is alluding to the classical Modernist Dutch artist Piet Mondrian, and Bauhaus motifs can be made out in the façade as well. But this figure, too, moves into the formal thinking of the postmodern era with the symmetry aspects that have already been mentioned, a pre-existing ground plan figure and formal motifs like a diagonal roof section.

Khareghat and Associates are using elements of a timeless language of classical Modernism in their attempt to combine Western, essentially rational abstraction with the Eastern abstraction of pre-figurative geometry. In Indian spiritual thinking geometry plays the principal part as the expression of a universal language not devised by mankind. In this way, even a high-rise apartment block gains a transcendental dimension, is "charged," as it were. This represents an interesting attempt of combining East and West, which also shows why purely functionalistic Modernism never really managed to make any headway into India. These captivating, symbolic buildings with their pleasing lucidity are urban signals of India's new self-confidence and self-awareness.

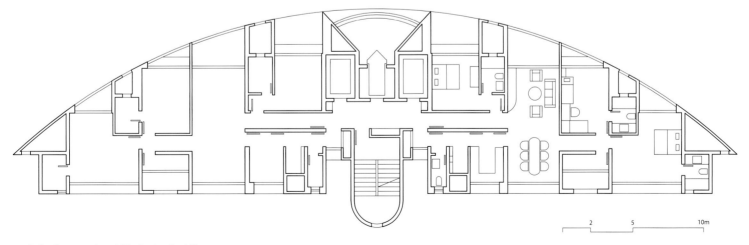

Belvedere apartment block, standard floor

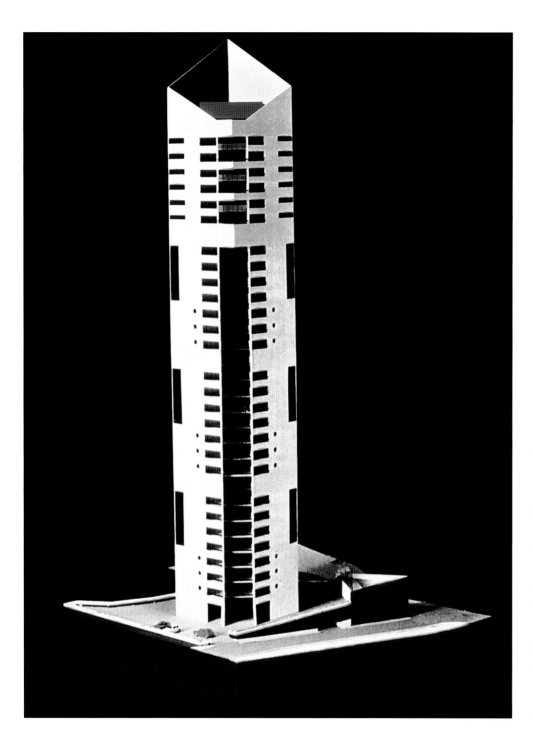
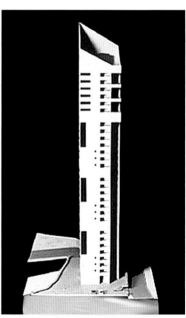

Tytan apartment block, different views

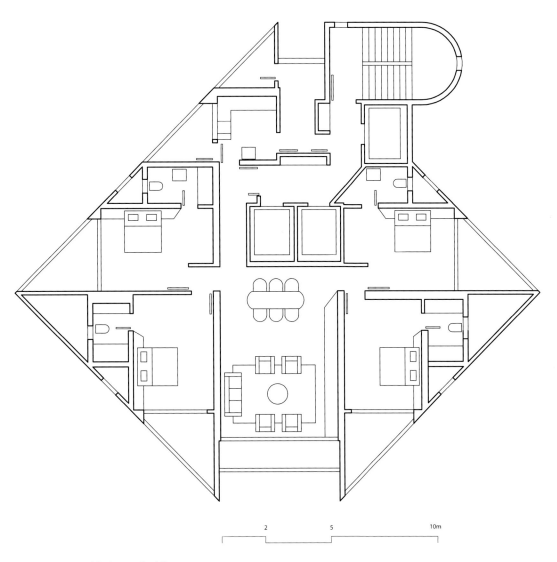

Tytan apartment block, standard floor

View of the house from the drive — Carport entrance

Kerala, the land of the coconut, is in the far south of India on the west coast, not far from the equator. This tropical palm garden, lavishly provided with natural green, is blessed with a constant temperature of 27 to 30°C, which can cool down to 20°C for short periods in the monsoon period from June to September. Cochin is a townscape with dense foliage penetrating as far as the centre in places, right on the sea and distributed over a number of "islands", an area crisscrossed by the backwaters, the natural channels immediately behind the coastline. These shallow waterways are all linked with the sea and are home to a great wealth of fish. The Leslie Pallath House is south of Cochin in a rural village area at the confluence of four canals, so that a kind of 3km wide lake is formed on the west side, towards the sea. The starting point for this design was a very long, narrow plot widening out slightly towards the water. The climatic and local conditions had to be considered, along with the client's express wish that all the bedrooms and living rooms should face the water. Other requirements were four bedrooms with their own bathrooms plus guest toilet, and an extraordinarily large kitchen with a separate work area. The function zones were thus divided classically into a kitchen and a living area, with a guest apartment on the ground floor and a bedroom area on the top floor. As a study was needed in combination with the master bedroom, the result was a structured space in the parents' area and a children's area on the top floor.

An entrance patio leads to a two-storey hall, the only vertical space, connecting the different levels and creating concentricity. The staircase opens into the hall, but remains essentially separate as a part of the building. The hall locates the soul of the house, and at the same time provides the focal point for a view over the whole length of the site to the driveway. From here it is possible to grasp the structured sectors of the plot: drive and parking for cars to the end of the carport and then the garden, featuring the lively line of a covered walk to the house. A framed aperture rising through two storeys illustrates the position of the hall for the outside world, a reference point for visitors and viewers. Framed in this way as protection against the sun and rain, it makes an impact outside as part of the building, but at the same time merges with the working area in the kitchen, which projects, single-storeyed, at the periphery. This creates an indentation in the otherwise flat, large entrance façade, an effect continued by a broad horizontal aperture at roof level. The roofed terrace with its umbrella-like sunscreen, spanning almost the entire house to keep out the heat, is at this level. This is a roof that does not detach itself, but becomes one again in the overall volume, along with the staircase figure. This roofed terrace is a place for an intense experience of nature, taking in all the outdoor scents and noises, a kind of living room outside the house.

The double, framed opening for the hall also reveals depth of volume, even allowing the surface of the water on the opposite side to shine through. The very narrow lighting and ventilation slit is created by the stairs, which protrude slightly as a result but is still blend with the lines of the main body of the building. It makes for a façade composition which sets

View from the water side

— Klaus-Peter Gast
House Leslie Pallath
Cochin (Kerala), 2005

View of the drive — View of the side entrance to the kitchen

into an almost contradictory relationship both flat expanse and great depth and effectively vertical and also horizontal sub-figures. Individual elements assert themselves, but are immediately "sucked into" the entirety of the overall volume. The long sides of the building are almost completely closed, it addresses the water side, appropriately to the spectacular view. Here, in contrast to the entrance side, a display window façade opens over both floors and embraces the full breadth of the house at door height, allowing an unbroken view of the water and the landscape. A dominant horizontal quality, structured by alternately closed parapet fields, is created by large, projecting balconies as terrace roofing and by rain shields across the entire breadth, with an umbrella roof that clearly projects on this side. A single column approximately a third of the way across the façade, supporting part of the load of a floor suspender beam, ties the projecting horizontal planes of the façade back into the cubature. That the cubic volume is markedly broken up on the water side is thus covered up, and the façade components are reintegrated into the mass of the body.

The design theme for the house is a stereometric, originally square solid, which is then distorted by added volume that is reintegrated within the two-dimensional aspects in order to create a sculptural effect. The white colour is chosen so that the body of the building with its flat rendered areas stands out as a homogeneous entity, reflecting the omnipresent sunlight in contrast to the natural green all around it. This formal vocabulary, borrowed from classical Modernism, also reminds of the high-quality Indian Modern movement that developed all over the country in the mid 1930s, peaking in subsequent years in the extraordinarily remarkable architecture of Indian Art Deco. This is some of the best work that Indian Modernism ever produced, and can still be found in rudimentary form in many towns throughout the country.

The overall ground plan and façade composition of the house, oscillating between rigidity and movement, is marked by classically balanced proportions that are in fact entirely appropriate to Indian Modernism. There they emerged from classical Indian architecture: Indian Modernism with its geometry and ordering structures sought to combine history with Modernism. The element of timelessness in this design approach embodied by this house is intended to be reminiscent of classical Indian Modernism it sets in where it left of and acts as a stimulus for developing it further.

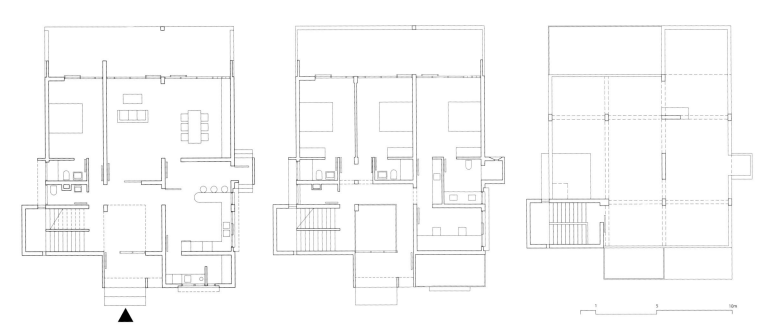

Ground floor — First floor — Roof-deck

Entrance loggia

View from the waterside

Gallery and stairs — View of the entrance side from the gallery

Side view with staircase

House Leslie Pallath

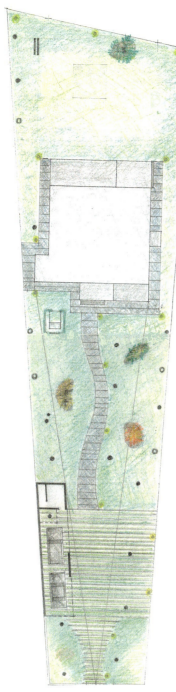

Garden and carport

Covered roof terrace ⎯ Kitchen entrance with shower area above

View of the entrance side with wind towers — Rear overview with view of the countryside

The complex planned by Rahul Mehrotra and his colleagues to accommodate the Tata Institute of Social Sciences (TISS) is in the remote hinterland of Maharashtra State. This extensive site, hilly in places, determined the most important aspects of the design through its character and conditions. The project consists of a group of three individual buildings: two provide accommodation with a catering area, arranged around a sophisticated courtyard. This takes up a typical and important motif of local settlements, the courtyard as an assembly and communication area, a place to spend the cooler evening hours. The communal outdoor area is a focal point for the Indians' intense interactive life, encouraging people to be together and developing into an open-air living room. This building brief in particular, accommodation for students in unaccustomed, strange and remote surroundings, had to take into consideration the idea of a central place for people to come together. The basic theme of an institution for social sciences also had to be reflected in the design, thus an emphasis on social life became part of the programme.

Two approximately square buildings, one for women and one for men, are placed opposite each other, both linked and separated by a courtyard of the same dimensions. Their entrances face the courtyard, and there are wide courtyards in the centre of each building providing light and access. A third square, only slightly larger, accommodates the eating area with kitchen facilities attached. It closes the courtyard, but is shifted off the axis by a clear distance. This opens the courtyard up to the countryside at one corner, though it is still framed by a wall running around it. Thus the surrounding countryside is not excluded, there is no intention to create a monastery, but it can be seen from the courtyard and becomes a component within its perspective. Classical axiality is also avoided, and above all is the kitchen pushed as close to the periphery as possible. The shifts suggest movement, an element that seems entirely appropriate in this sloping landscape. Mehrotra establishes a sense of symmetry at the main entrance to the courtyard, but this is cancelled out again by the run of the terrain and the staggered building line arising from it. Two exciting, contrary directions are created, with and against the slope, which means that the second main theme, the topography, can always be perceived physically. The architect also plays with the volumes: an outer wall fuses the individual buildings together so that a coherent, staggered line of wall "flows down" the slope. This "oneness" is divided into three parts only on the inside, but a sense of unity is still maintained. Here Mehrotra is expressively articulating the topographical situation through the architecture, making it part of the building. There is no moment of radical intervention, like creating a plateau, for example, but the site is accepted as status quo and indeed positively celebrated. Crystalline contours give way to softly flowing lines, the mildness of the slope opposes the rigidity of the geometry. The movement in the terrain is particularly visible in the central courtyard, with responding steps and frames as classical Indian exterior motifs, enhancing the courtyard to make it a space for experience.

But the courtyard has yet another remarkable function to perform: it regulates the climate. Air circulation and natural

—Rahul Mehrotra and Associates
Accommodation for the Tata Institute of Social Sciences
Tuljapur (Maharashtra), 2000

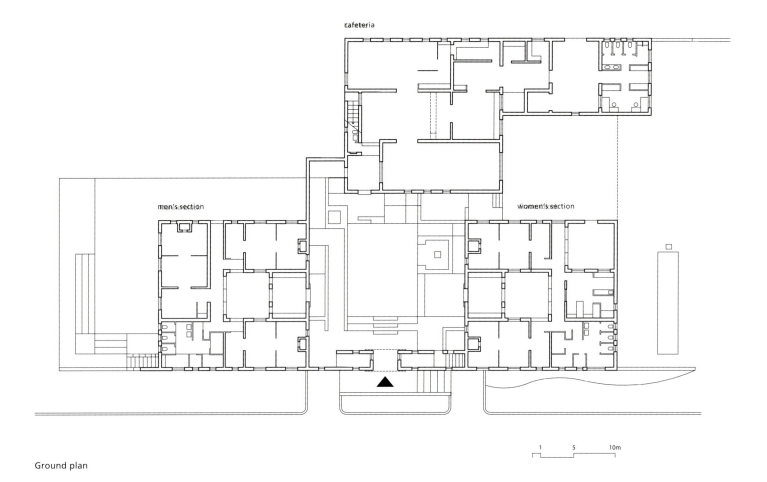

Ground plan

Situation of the complex in the countryside

cooling for rooms are crucial features of Indian planning, courtyards mean that air and light can be admitted indirectly. But Rahul Mehrotra takes up the existing air circulation on a hilly site and turns it into the highly dramatic and most impressive motif in the design: wind towers capture the wind at great height and carry it down their shafts into the rooms, above all the bedroom accommodation. This demonstrates an imaginative approach to the ecology of a building, using nature rather than the customary expensive solution of artificial climatisation. These wind-catchers are a motif from ancient Iranian cities that has been rediscovered, they make their own quite natural contribution to the building's air-conditioning. The materials for the group of buildings were also selected in terms of this aspect: locally available basalt became the dominant building material, because it was the only one available without requiring long transport distances. For the floors and ceilings the architect used cap-vault ceilings made of narrow lightweight concrete shells; these isolate very well, and can carry heavy loads, they also save material and are reasonably priced. The load-bearing walls are in heat-resistant basalt, set unrendered in their natural roughness, and these shape the overall appearance of the design. No plaster, no colour was used, but the surface of the stone, which looks lasting and durable, subject to very little change, guarantees long life without the need for continuous maintenance and restoration because of the long monsoon rains. The natural beauty of this black stone homogenises the complex as a whole, it ties all its parts together and expresses the design's ecological approach directly. It would scarcely be possible to find a better way to formulate such an intention aesthetically, and it would also be scarcely possible to use the local conditions better. But the poetry of Rahul Mehrotra's design thrives on its contradictions: a horizontal flow of individual buildings, with vertical tower emphases; solid dimensions and slight movement; topographical response and artificial line; closed outside and spacious inside; geometrically rigid and fluid in motion. Also, the material conveys a feeling of protection, solidity, security and honesty. Associations with medieval fortresses are easily at hand with this solid-looking material and the formal language of a fixed base with tall towers, and this may indeed be a motif that influenced the design idea. The occupants feel thoroughly protected in this introverted residential complex with ecological features and expressive, almost symbolic material.

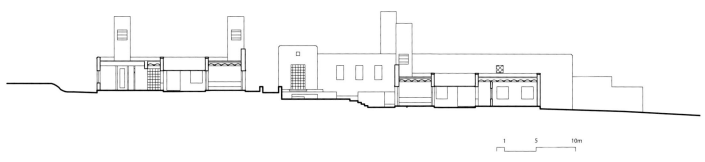

Section

Inner courtyard — Inner courtyard with main entrance and wind towers

Accommodation for the Tata Institute of Social Sciences

Inner courtyard with main entrance — Inner courtyard with view of the main entrance

In the dwelling area

Accommodation for the Tata Institute of Social Sciences

View of a dwelling area's inner courtyard — Corridor in a dwelling area

The closed west side ― View of the main entrance on the east side

TRADITIONAL

This four-storey building is inside a cramped, densely developed suburb of Mumbai, surrounded by multi-storey apartment blocks. The architect Shimul Javeri Kadri and her colleagues (this is an all-female architecture practice) were faced with the particular challenge of dealing with a narrow plot only 16m wide. As the building was to be a clinic, there also had to be 4m between the building and the street on both sides, so that that finally there were only 8m available. But this rule applied only to the ground floor, and so it was possible to skilfully create the additional space needed on the other floors with protruding balconies and external closed supply shafts.

The brief lays down a complex programme: the main entrance is on the ground floor with a passage-like corridor opening up to the outside world, plus cafeteria, kitchen and shop. Here the building is still very public. The first floor contains the large waiting area and the adjacent consulting room for three assistant doctors and the two principal doctors. Above this, on the second floor, are the treatment rooms, which are designed for use of the special, traditional old Indian method of treatment using nothing but purely natural medicaments, called Ayurveda. These rooms were intended to make the treatments associated with this approach possible, and needed a special technical equipment for automatically supplying high-quality oils and other fats. As in the two storeys below, the east side of the building, which faces away from the monsoon, opens up towards a passage. The third floor with large closed balconies on the west side was intended for in-patients, wards with double and single beds linked to an open terrace by a centrally placed corridor.

The overall appearance of the building is both fascinating and disturbing, as both the façades and the interior are characterised by traditional architectural elements. There is a severe set of structural piers, but these run out into areas of light-coloured rendering and thus remain definitely "modern." The secondary architecture is dominant: protruding roofs in carefully detailed traditional timber structures with visible brick cladding; pre-existing timber posts with carved base and capital decoration; old wooden windows with wooden shutters; Venetian blinds and profiled frames from anonymous buildings of the past; richly ornamented doors in fine woods and elaborate door-furnishings with frame figures and stone plinths from buildings of earlier centuries that were undoubtedly significant. But there are also round double pillars, a steel spiral staircase, modern window frames and furniture from both the past and the present. The architect blends forms from different times and style with great virtuosity, combines found old material with carefully selected new items and tries to let the material quality of the parts speak for itself. The use of natural material with natural surfaces brings out the different inherent tactile qualities. It is clearly the wish of its users and builders to succeed with genuine nature. This is where the special aesthetic fascination of this building lies, illustrating the significance of the ancient Ayurveda for our days, in architectural terms, in its combination of modern structure and historical elements. A traditional architectural pictorial language is placed alongside

Situation of the building in the quarter

—Shimul Javeri Kadri Architects
Ayushakti – Ayurvedic Treatment Clinic
Mumbai (Maharashtra), 1999

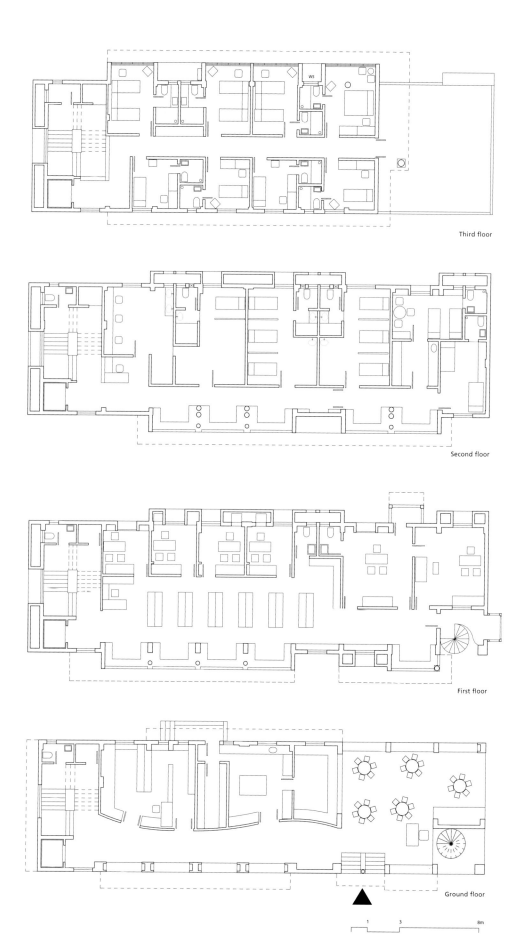

Ground floor to third floor plan

the traditional method of treatment, allegories suggest something unchangeable, timeless, permanently valid. The old is not being imitated here, nothing is prettified, everything old remains authentic, with the value of its ageing process, its patina, its particular qualities, its craftsmanship and its decoration. It remains a true witness to the past. In this new context the old suddenly becomes modern, with new weight and significance, breaking the abstract harshness of Modernism without devaluing it. The modern load-bearing elements also follow the honesty of the traditional construction methods used here. The lucidity of the load-bearing structure is emphasised, but it gains an almost autonomous character from the multiplicity of pillar types, gaining a life of its own.

One striking feature of this building is an inclination towards gentleness in the choice of attributes, with curved walls on the ground floor, appealing colours, playful details like arches and decoration and an atmosphere of warmth. It is not least this that shows a trait that is perhaps feminine in this design from an all-woman practice.

Given the intention of integrating typical India building components, of course a typically Indian atmosphere comes to the fore, and as has already been said, it seems entirely appropriate for its purpose. Frequently parts like this are applied to tourist buildings in India, superficially, folksily and decoratively, and thus degenerating into kitsch. Shimul Javeri Kadri and her team have solved this particular problem superbly, for an Indian clientele at a typically ordinary Indian location. And this, too, makes their intentions particularly credible.

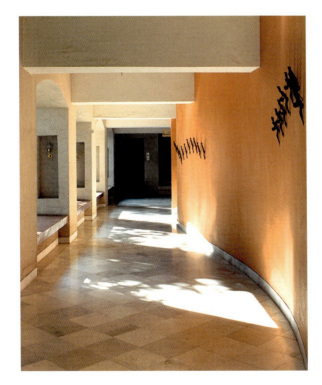

Views of the ground floor passage

Exit to the third floor roof terrace — The loggia for the second floor waiting area

Openings of the entrance side ⌐ Spiral staircase on the ground floor ⌐ Integration of a traditional door ⌐ In the cafeteria

General view — Panorama

George Brunton, a 19th century British shipbuilder, had a yard directly at the Fort Cochin harbour entrance in the old, historical part of the town, where the Portuguese explorer Vasco da Gama, who discovered the sea route to India, was once buried. This plot had been derelict for a long time and was then acquired by the owners of the Experience Hotel cgh earth, so that they could build a new hotel in this part of the city, which is very attractive for tourists. The hotel was intended to provide a breathtaking view over this harbour entrance. The difficult part of the task was adding a new building to this characterful part of the old town that would do justice to the existing shore development ensemble, but still remain self-confident. Fort Cochin, with its few remaining fragments of a star-shaped bastion, is now a museum for centuries of European colonisation: first the Portuguese, then the Dutch and lastly the British fought each other for supremacy, leaving clear traces of the struggle. It is still possible to discern traces of Portuguese Baroque, mainly in the façades of the old churches, but some surviving private houses also show evidence of pointed-arched Gothic masonry combined with Dutch-Indian hipped roof structures. But all these diverse imports from Europe joined to bring the townscape together under one roof, as it were: the steep-pitched roof, often hipped and combined with typical Indian gable ventilation and usually with a uniform tile covering, dominated the overall look of the town.

Karl Damschen, the German-Swiss architect of the Brunton Boatyard Hotel, treated history and the town's current appearance as a spur for developing his design along these historical lines. Damschen, who has been commuting between Bern and Cochin with his wife since 1981, has internalised the genius loci, the spirit of the place, and found it a very satisfying task to preserve historical stock and to conduct urban repair. He sees his hotel design as a project of this kind, closing a gap in the town's development, and at the same time critises the unthinking removal of old buildings in favour of new buildings of absolutely no merit. He wanted to express "the value of the old in a new building" (Damschen).

The design consists of an ensemble of three individual buildings combined by a courtyard into a rectangular figure, and thus forming a unit. A lavish but single-storey L-shaped building on the street side contains reception area and lounge. One special feature of this space is that on two sides, facing the drive and the garden courtyard, it has no glazing. It is furnished with benches, chests and café tables in the old style, and represents a pleasant, semi-open transition from street space to hotel room. Here, Damschen incorporates an interesting element from the pre-electric period, punkas, i.e. fans operated mechanically by cables. The reception hall reaches up to the top of the ridge, leaving the wonderful wooden structure of the roof visible, with the fans acting as articulating elements below. Terracotta tiles and seating niches in the openings in red, polished cement oxide are well-considered details in a carefully selected combination of materials. A central protruding section with an added platform leads to the courtyard behind reception, then articulates the long building. To the left of the entrance, the L-figure

Entrance

Karl Damschen
Brunton Boatyard Hotel
Cochin (Kerala), 1999

Lake view ⌐ Lake side

completes itself as U in the form of a two-storey restaurant section with kitchen on the ground floor and the main restaurant above. This is attractive not just because of the interior décor, completely in wood and with visible roof truss, but above all because of the all-round glazing in wooden window frames, their structure concealing the wooden load-bearing columns. This section of the building reveals the motif that shapes the whole design: a mezzanine floor entirely in dark wood under the roof zone, covered with a widely projecting hipped roof. A motif from the Dutch colonial period is being quoted here, one that still crops up on historical buildings in a lot of places in Kerala. The massive, white-rendered main body of the building rises to the parapet area of this floor as a kind of base, with the filigree-looking timber construction sitting on top of it as a "crown" with the roof. Thus this floor is reduced visually, creating the impression that it actually already is the roof zone. Karl Damschen now uses this trick as well in the main section of the hotel, a two-storey base building with a third floor in the form of a timber mezzanine.

The H-shaped figure faces the water symmetrically. It contains 22 rooms and four suites in the protruding corner projections. The sections together form a calm, garden courtyard zone, a balanced rectangle, in which a venerable Portuguese import has been carefully preserved, a Brazilian rain tree whose enormous crown provides shade for the courtyard. The access loggias for the rooms run along this courtyard, as the hotel has rooms on only one side of the building, meaning that all the rooms as well as all the bathrooms face the sea. Damschen says that the owner was happy to accept the loss of additional rooms, as he realised straight away the particular attraction for the mainly foreign guests. In this way, Damschen also avoids the usual shaft-like entrance area between bathroom and hanging area that is otherwise customary, gaining a little foyer in each room. The large hipped roof with its deeply shaded mezzanine area looks particularly impressive on this long, peacefully grounded building. Its white base is broken up by loggias – with flat arches on the ground floor – while the protruding sections acquire slender vertical apertures with round arches striving upwards. Thus more solid mass remains at the ends of the building, which necessarily has to support the large roof in a way that is visually convincing as well.

Karl Damschen's design makes a new building part of a highly sensitive urban structure. It looks perfectly natural, but enriches the scene extraordinarily. Its careful ties with tradition are credible; they interpret what is there, accepting valuable everyday motifs in a mature city. This is not Postmodern quotation making the design seem timeless, but a disciplined modern retention of order, with great reticence in the formal elements. Thus the Indian colonial heritage of the place is not just honoured, but continued in an unusual way.

Lobby — Reception

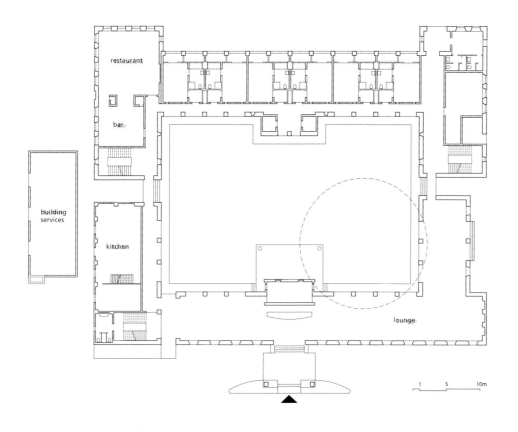

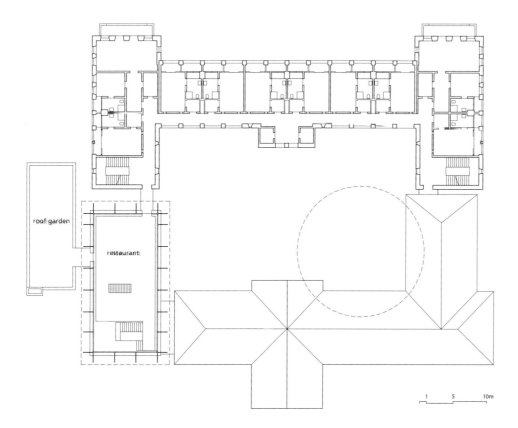

Ground floor plan — First floor plan

Corridor on the second floor

Restaurant on the first floor ⎯ Café ⎯ Hotel room

Loggia on the second floor　Inner courtyard

Full view of the complex

Circle centre through a wide-angle lens

ECOLOGICAL-SUSTAINABLE

A growing awareness of ecology, economics and sustainability in building led to the idea of developing a centre for innovative materials, systems and processes. It was commissioned by the Confederation of Indian Industry (CII), an industrial association that wanted a so-called technology centre for exhibition purposes, an auditorium, conference rooms and library for discussion and the exchange of ideas, and an office area. Karan Grover and Associates had to tackle the far from simple task of applying this entirely new building industry approach to a structure that addressed all these key points. Of course ecological and economic building methods were to be used, but also the building itself should communicate the new approach when one simply looked at it, thus drawing attention to itself by signalling its intentions. The building was to set new standards for the future in sustainable ecological building, and thus acquire model character. The outcome was the Green Business Center, a place for new ideas for the new user, the Green Building Council. To convey this message was one challenge for the architects, but the shape of the building of course also depended on the specific conditions imposed by the client, the place and the situation.

The architects' key idea was to create a structure whose characteristics expressed the "energy aesthetic," an organism that tries to benefit from the efficiency of natural structures without imitating them. This building was intended as an attractive advertisement for the Green movement, which is slowly gaining a hold in India, loudly proclaiming the message needed for the future. A generous building plot made it possible to realise the idea of a structure circling around a centre without too much difficulty, with the structure itself consisting of different circle radii. The actual centre remains empty: this is the energy centre, also the communication centre, an open courtyard, the axis mundi, the axis of creation. The centre creates a centrifugal effect, parts of the design spring apart, try to escape from the centre, but are caught and held together again by a bracket, a round canopy over the connecting route. Opposing forces create a kind of dynamic tension, ultimately the sense of drifting apart is held in check. It is quite clear that the components of the design can be distinguished in terms of function and presented as individual parts: the auditorium and the technology centre face each other as large circle radii smaller conference rooms attempt to forge a connection, and the office and service sections stand as special bodies outside these radii but remain fixed components of the composition. The centre collects and binds within this exploded geometry, while the periphery softens, a finding of form based on nature phenomena. The heterogeneous nature of the sub-figures is interestingly relativised here: everything acquires rounded edges, soft forms, and thus forms a closer association again. There is also no split between inside and outside, the centre is definitely connected to the area outside.

This constellation of the various parts produces aspects that do justice to the building's ecological claims: the circular form minimises the surface of the walls, which are exposed to enormous heat; this also minimises the floor area figure, guaranteeing maximum retention of open and green areas.

—Karan Grover and Associates
Sohrabji Godrej Green Business Center
Hyderabad (Andhra Pradesh), 2003

Courtyard and gallery ⌐ Semi-transparent grille walls

The roof areas are covered with soil and greenery, a relatively simple way of keeping out heat, as no elaborate insulation is needed. It was important to retain the natural soil base and to avoid soil erosion through a correct response to the nature of the subsoil, thus local flora and fauna were retained and encouraged as soil-enriching factors. For example, it was important to examine the soil for water content, as the way it runs is important, and not just for Hindus, but as well in terms of supply and for the underground flow of forces. The land has often been dried up by improper building measures as a result of lack of attention, and is a significant mistake in this heat-tormented country. A natural sculptural feature, the existence of rock in the subsoil, became an attractive component of the complex and was included in the green planning. Water use in the toilets was optimised so that water was handled with due care; the urinals do not use water, for example. Soiled water is filtered through natural systems and can partially be re-used. Construction materials were chosen after making careful comparisons: insulation values for different masonry types and roof coverings were examined and optimised, windows were given double glazing with an argon filling, largely a novelty in India, and the position and dimensions of the windows was calculated very thoroughly in terms of need and points of the compass. Even the rubbish reduction in the manufacturing process for the windows was a calculated part of the ecological process. Dazzling light, which usually also contributes to overheating in sections of a building, was avoided by the use of grille-like brick walls. These create a screening effect as walls in front of a building or as boundaries in a courtyard. They create dazzle-free light very simply and also last for a long time. Of course natural lighting was to play the principal part in lighting the interior, despite all the other considerations. In isolated cases it was complemented with additional skylights, but was also achieved by lavish glazing on the north side of the auditorium foyer. The complex has 90% natural light controlled by sensors, enormously reducing the electrical energy requirements arising from artificial light. Avoiding atmospheric pollution was another priority; even air pollution by machines like photocopiers was dealt with by filter systems. CO_2 sensors were installed and the whole area declared a smoke-free zone. Absolutely no toxic materials were to be used, particularly inside the building, so that the climate in the rooms would not be compromised in any way. A high proportion of material re-use was also taken into consideration when planning the building. Materials were not to be brought in from further afar than 500 km, to keep the transport costs down. Solar energy is central to the energy supply, and photovoltaic cells were installed over almost the full area of the technology centre roof. But another natural element that was very important on the spot here was to be used successfully as well: wind energy, not to supply electricity, but to save it when cooling the rooms. Wind towers introduce the natural high air currents into the rooms, thus keeping the interior climate comfortable at almost no cost.

The Green Business Center is one of the first consistent attempts in India to take advantage of the natural features of a location for the building work, and to make effective and efficient energy use in the building part of the design. These efforts were rewarded with a "Platinum Classification," the highest award of the US Green Building Council, based on international standards. The building's self-confident, extraordinary form embues it with a symbolic power to radiate and become a stimulus and support for the Indian Green movement across as wide a field as possible.

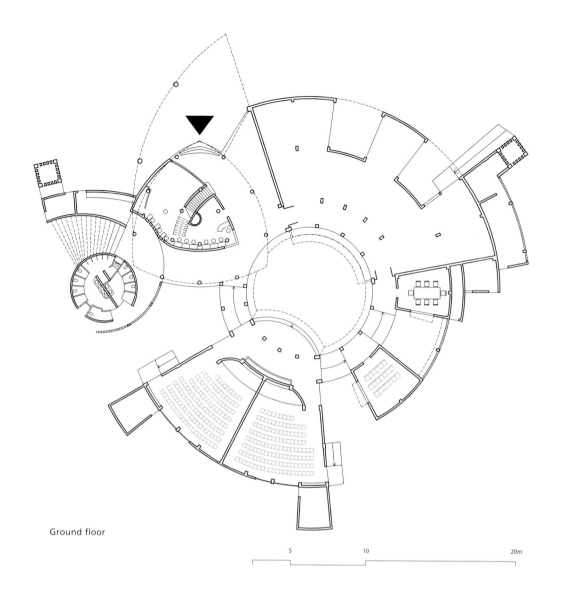

Ground floor

Between office and technology centre — Steps to the centre

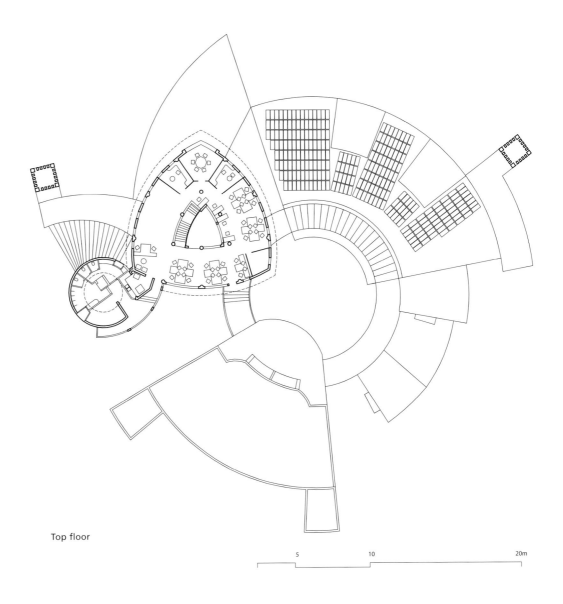

Top floor

5　　　10　　　20m

Gallery with view of the office building — Gallery pillars

In the technology centre hall

Technology centre hall — Furniture

Main entrance — View of the main entrance

Left wind tower, centre offices with service area and auditorium on the right

Wind tower

Selected Bibliography

Bahga, Sarabjit: Modern Architecture in India, New Delhi 1993
Bhatia, Gautam: Punjabi Baroque and Other Memories of Architecture, New Delhi 1994
Bhatia, Gautam: Silent Spaces And Other Stories of Architecture, New Delhi 1994
Bhatt, Vikram; Scriver, Peter: Contemporary Indian Architecture. After the Masters, Ahmedabad 1990
Bubbar, Darshan: The Spirit of Indian Architecture, Mumbai 2005
Chatterjee, Malay: The Evolution of Contemporary Indian Architecture. Paris 1985
Correa, Charles; Frampton, Kenneth (foreword): The Works of Charles Correa, Mumbai 1996
Curtis, William: The Ancient in the Modern, Paris 1985
Deshpandi, R.: Modern Homes for India, Poona 1948 (1939)
Dwivedi, Sharada; Mehrotra, Rahul: Bombay. The Cities Within, Mumbai 1995
Evenson, Norma: The Indian Metropolis. The View Towards the West, New Delhi 1989
Gast, Klaus-Peter: Louis I. Kahn. The Idea of Order, Basel, Berlin, Boston 1998
Gast, Klaus-Peter: Le Corbusier. Paris-Chandigarh, Basel, Berlin, Boston 2000
Ghirardo, Diane: Architecture After Modernism, London 1996
Grover, Satish: Building Beyond Borders. The Story of Contemporary Indian Architecture, New Delhi 1995
Jain, Uttam: Modern Architecture in India, Mumbai 1991
Joglekar, M.N.; Das, S.K.: Contemporary Indian Architecture. Housing and Urban Development, New Delhi 1995
Joshi, Kiran: Documenting Chandigarh. The Indian Architecture of Pierre Jeanneret, Maxwell Fry and Jane Drew, Ahmedabad 1999
Kalia, Ravi: Chandigarh. In Search of an Identity, Carbondale 1987
Khan, Hasan-Uddin: Charles Correa, Singapore 1987
Khosla, Romi: Current Architecture in India, Mimar 41, 1991
Krishnan, Arvind: Climate Responsible Architecture, New Delhi 2000
Lang, Jon: A Concise History of Modern Architecture in India, New Delhi 2002
Le Corbusier: The Master Plan, II. The Capitol, Marg 15, p. 5–19, 1961
Mehrotra, Rahul; Nest, Günter: The Fort Precinct in Bombay. Conserving an Image Centre, Mumbai 1994
Michell, George; Martinelli, Antonio: The Royal Palaces of India, London 1994
Mitter, Partha: Art and Nationalism in Colonial India 1850–1922, Cambridge 1994
Nehru, Jawaharlal: The Discovery of India, New Delhi, 1947
Nilsson, Sten Ake: The New Capitals of India, Pakistan and Bangladesh, London 1973
Prasad, Sunand: Le Corbusier in India, Architecture + Design 3, S. 14–27, 1987
Prakash, Vikramaditya: Chandigarh. The City Beautiful, Chandigarh 1999
Rewal, Raj: Raj Rewal, Electa, Milan 1986
Rewal, Raj: Library for the Indian Parliament, New Delhi 2002
Sen, Amartya: The Argumentative Indian, London 2005
Tharoor, Shashi: India. From Midnight to the Millenium, New Delhi 2000
Tillotson, Giles H.: The Tradition of Indian Architecture. Continuity, Controversy and Change Since 1850, New Haven 1989

Illustration Credits

Daruwalla, Pallon 50, 52, 54, 55, 56, 57, 58, 59

Desai, Sachin 60 (top), 62 (top and bottom right), 63, 66, 67

Gast, Klaus-Peter 21 (right), 22 (top, middle and bottom left), 60 (bottom), 61, 62 (bottom left), 94 (bottom)

Gobai, Noshir 104, 105, 107, 108, 109

Jadhav, Raj 8 (top right and bottom right), 10 (right)

Jamese, Lijan 88, 89, 90, 92, 93, 94 (top)

Kurishingal, Tanya 20 (bottom), 110, 111, 112, 113, 115, 116, 117

Mehrotra, Rahul 96

Raj Rewal Associates 12 (bottom and middle)

Vora, Rajesh 34, 36, 38, 39, 40, 41, 98, 100, 101, 102, 103